Embroidery
& CROSS STITCH

Creative
EMBROIDERY

Craftworld Books

Contents

The crewel world unveiled ...

Embroidery is practised across the world and is one of the oldest of textile crafts. Today, the art of embroidery and cross stitch is again increasing in popularity – from ceremonial garments, both secular and ecclesiastical, to everyday clothes, carpets and household linen, embroidery has certainly left its mark. What started out as a practical measure has turned into a highly skilled way of embellishing furnishings, fabrics, garments and more.

Text by Melissa Habchi

The art of this elegant and timeless craft developed in different ways over long periods in various parts of the world.

In medieval Byzantium, court garments and religious vestments were embroidered in rich colours and ornate designs. In Greece from ancient times, linen panels

were embroidered in colourful silk, with geometric and floral patterns; in other parts of Europe, embroidery developed as a means of enriching clothing, church decorations, wall-hangings and domestic linens and furnishings.

During the Tudor era, embroidery prospered as a domestic craft. Working

furnishings for the great country houses became a major endeavour for the women of the household, and to be skilled with a needle was a vital accomplishment for a lady.

Chinese embroidery was principally used only to decorate garments for the elite, such as the celebrated and well-preserved robes of Chinese emperors adorned with traditional dragon motifs and other symbols of power, often worked on a dark silk.

By the 18th century, embroidery flourished throughout the world. In the east, the silk designs on Japanese kimonos displayed a level of skill hitherto unmatched, while in Europe, fashionable costumes for both men and women were decorated with fine embroidery.

The discovery of new lands led to an upsurge of interest in the exotic plants and flowers found there. As a result, images of these newly-discovered species were copied from books and adorned the gowns of wealthy courtiers.

During the 19th century, the Victorians practised and enjoyed a wide range of embroidery styles such as stunning samplers and exquisite alphabets. Fine and often exquisite white-on-white embroidery was used on underwear and household linens, and among the peasants and artisans, traditional techniques continued to be

popular and were passed on from one generation to the next.

The trends of the 20th century are also still around us. In the 1960s, British embroidery began an era of unprecedented development which saw the craft being taken seriously in colleges and schools. Skills have since developed even further and modern technology has produced such innovations as machine embroidery.

Interest in this ancient craft has continued into the new millennium. Today we have so much access to knowledge from the many cultures that have developed over the centuries – not to mention an extraordinary range of threads, needles, fabrics, books, patterns, videos and classes – so there is a never ending abundance of information to be found about this 'crewel' world.

Soft & Gentle

Teddy Bear Coathangers

Here's the perfect solution to your gift-giving problems.
Joan Watters' cute coathangers will appeal to any age group
and they don't take long to make.

PREPARATION

Cut your wool blanketing to the measurements shown on the pattern sheet (page 85). Trace your chosen design, marking the centre of each flower with a dot. Mark the top of the tracing.

Centre the tracing on the blanketing and pin it in place. Poke a hole with a needle at each dot and press your water-erasable pen firmly through them to transfer the design to the blanketing.

EMBROIDERY

Garlanded bear coathanger: Work the mauve Stem-stitch roses first. Draw a small circle of about 12mm (¹⁄₂in) around the dot. Thread the No 20 chenille needle with double mauve mohair and, starting with a knot, stitch a row of Stem Stitches

very loosely around the circle. Work a second row of Stem Stitches inside the first row and then work a third row. The last stitch in the rose is a loose loop in the centre. Finish off the thread securely.

Work the Colonial-knot rosebuds in double mauve mohair, then embroider the stems with a single strand of green mohair, working a very small Fly Stitch around the bud and extending the holding stitch back to the rose as a stem.

Still using the green mohair, add the rose leaves by working two Fly Stitches, one inside the other, and finishing with a Straight Stitch extending from the centre of the Fly Stitch.

Work the Feather-stitch vine next, using cream Perlé Cotton. Finish with two Lazy Daisy-stitch leaves at the bottom of the vine and extend the holding stitches a little more than usual.

Using the No 10 crewel needle, sew on three cream Mill Hill seed beads at the end of each spoke of the Feather Stitch. Hand-sew the bear button in place.

MATERIALS

- 2, 48cm x 12cm (19in x 5in) pieces of wool blanketing
- Adult-size wooden coathanger
- 10cm x 150cm (4in x 59in) wadding
- Scraps of satin rouleau to cover coathanger hook
- 1m x 3mm (1¹⁄₈yd x ¹⁄₈in) cream double-sided satin ribbon
- 30cm x 1cm (12in x ¹⁄₂in) cream double-sided satin ribbon
- 1m x 4cm (1¹⁄₈yd x 1¹⁄₂in) cream pre-gathered lace with eyelet holes
- No 9 and 10 crewel needles
- 20 chenille needle
- Cream sewing thread
- Water-erasable pen: blue
- Tracing paper, pencil

GARLANDED BEAR COATHANGER

- Teddy bear button with mauve flower garland
- DMC Cotton Perlé No 5: 1 skein cream (846)
- Kacoonda hand-dyed mohair: 1 skein Special Mauve
- Little Wood Fleece hand-dyed mohair: 1 skein blue/green
- Mill Hill glass seed beads: 1 packet cream (00123)

ANGEL BEAR COATHANGER

- Teddy bear angel button
- DMC Perlé Cotton No 5: 1 skein ecru
- DMC Stranded Embroidery Cotton: 1 skein ecru
- Paterna Tapestry wool: 1 skein each of cream (263), very pale apricot (805), olive green (643)
- Small amount of gold thread and Candlelight Rainbow thread
- Mill Hill glass pebble beads: 6, cream (05147)
- Mill Hill glass seed beads: 1 packet cream (00123)

STITCHES USED

Stem Stitch, Colonial Knot, Fly Stitch, Straight Stitch, Feather Stitch, Lazy Daisy Stitch, Buttonhole Stitch

You may find it necessary to add an extra stitch around the bear's neck to hold it more firmly.

For a personal touch, finish with your initials and the year.

Angel bear coathanger: Embroider roses, buds and leaves in the same manner as for the Garlanded bear coathanger. Use double Paterna wool in cream and pale apricot for the roses, positioning them as shown in the photograph. The leaves are worked in a single strand of green wool.

The vine is stitched in continuous Fly Stitch, using Perlé thread. Work a Colonial Knot on the end of each spoke of the Fly Stitch using the Candlelight Rainbow thread doubled.

Stitch on the teddy bear angel button using gold thread. You may find it necessary to add an extra stitch around the bear's neck to hold it securely. Embroider the bear's halo using gold thread and Buttonhole Stitch worked in a small circle.

Hanging berries: Measure and cut 127cm (50in) of stranded cotton. Separate one strand and thread the No 10 crewel needle. Take one pebble bead and bring the needle through the centre hole, leaving about 20cm (8in) of thread hanging. Go over the bead and through the hole until the bead is completely covered, threading on three seed beads just before you take the last thread through the hole in the pebble bead. The tail that is left is used to sew the berry onto the fabric.

Make five more berries in the same way. Sew three at the top of each Fly-stitch vine. Thread the No 9 crewel needle with the two tail threads of a berry and sew it to the right side of the fabric, leaving about a 12mm ($^1/_2$in) stem so that it hangs down. Work Buttonhole Stitch along the stem.

Before making up, initial and date your finished embroidery.

MAKING UP

❖

Overlock the bottom edge only of each piece of blanketing and machine-sew the lace onto the overlocked edge. If the pre-gathered lace has eyelet holes for ribbon, you can now thread the ribbon through then hand-sew the bow in place.

Screw the metal hook into the wooden coathanger and wrap the wadding around the hanger twice, securing the end with a few stitches.

Slide the satin rouleau over the hook of the hanger and hand-stitch it securely to the wadding. Turn the other end of the rouleau inside and stitch it closed.

Place the embroidered and backing blanketing pieces right sides together and, allowing a 4mm ($^1/_8$in) seam allowance, machine-sew around the outside edge. Leave a 3-4mm ($^1/_8$in) opening at the centre of the top to slide the hanger hook through. Do not sew along the lace edge.

Turn the blanketing to the right side and slip it over the coathanger, then hand-sew the two pieces of blanketing together at the bottom edge. ❁

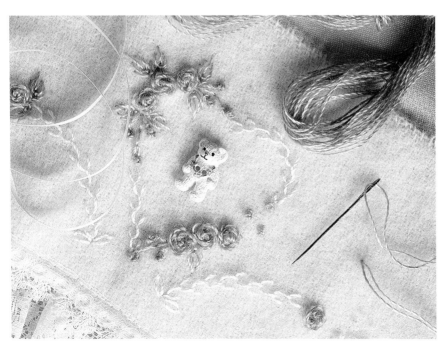

The Secret Garden

This petit point design of an Eastern palace with its secret garden will appeal to all those who love mystique and fantasy. It is designed and stitched by Marie Larkin using stranded embroidery cotton in rich, jewel-like colours.

MATERIALS

- 40cm x 30cm (16in x 12in) white, antique white or cream 25-count Dublin linen

- DMC Stranded Embroidery Cotton: 1 skein each of light lavender (211), very dark blue green (500), medium blue green (503), very dark violet (550), medium violet (552), very dark cranberry (600), plum (718), light garnet (814), medium burnt orange (946), dark teal blue (3808), medium teal blue (3809)

- DMC Stranded Rayon: 1 skein gold (30972)

- No 26 tapestry needle

- 15cm (6in) embroidery hoop

STITCHES USED

Half Cross Stitch, French Knots, Couching, Straight Stitch

FINISHED SIZE

12cm x 7cm (4³/₄in x 2³/₄in)

PREPARATION

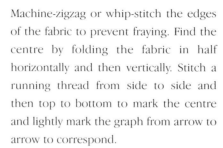

Machine-zigzag or whip-stitch the edges of the fabric to prevent fraying. Find the centre by folding the fabric in half horizontally and then vertically. Stitch a running thread from side to side and then top to bottom to mark the centre and lightly mark the graph from arrow to arrow to correspond.

STITCHING

❖

Each square on the chart represents a Half Cross Stitch worked diagonally over one thread. The symbols in the squares indicate the colours to use.

When working with cotton, use three strands, and when working an area in rayon, use two strands. Separate the threads and allow them to untwist before threading the needle. This makes the stitches sit flat and gives a better texture to the finished work.

Begin stitching from the centre of the design, but not with a knot as it will be visible when your work is framed. To start a new thread, bring the needle from the back of the fabric through to the front, leaving a short tail of thread on the wrong side. Hold this tail against the fabric and secure it with the first few stitches. To end off a thread, weave it through the back of several stitches to hold it in place. Avoid carrying threads across the back of your embroidery as they can show through the fabric.

In this design, the colours are worked in defined blocks, making it simple to complete one colour area before moving on to the next.

Working the embroidery in a hoop will give better tension, but do not leave it in the hoop when you are not working

on it, as this can leave marks that are difficult to remove.

SPECIAL INSTRUCTIONS

❖

The wall beside the steps is stitched using two strands of very dark violet (550), together with one strand of light garnet (814).

When stitching the pond, miss every alternate stitch on each alternate row, staggering the missed stitch each time to create the pattern.

The flagpoles on the tall minarets are worked in Straight Stitch and then Couched using gold 30972.

When all the stitching has been completed, scatter the French Knot oranges randomly on the trees in the garden.

FINISHING

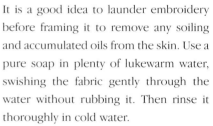

It is a good idea to launder embroidery before framing it to remove any soiling and accumulated oils from the skin. Use a pure soap in plenty of lukewarm water, swishing the fabric gently through the water without rubbing it. Then rinse it thoroughly in cold water.

Roll the wet embroidery in a dry towel and apply gentle pressure to remove the excess water. Place the damp embroidery right side down on a dry white towel, cover it with an ironing cloth and press it lightly. Do not apply any pressure with the iron as this will flatten the stitches. Carefully lay the embroidery out flat and leave it overnight to dry completely.

Your beautiful embroidery is now ready for framing.

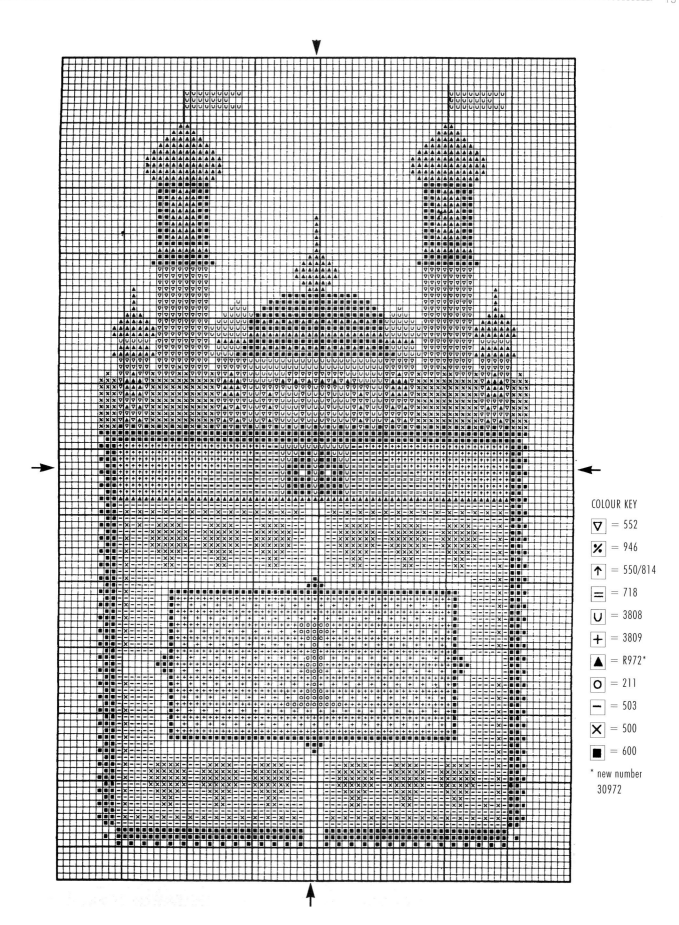

COLOUR KEY

▽ = 552

✗ = 946

↑ = 550/814

= = 718

U = 3808

+ = 3809

▲ = R972*

O = 211

— = 503

✕ = 500

■ = 600

* new number
30972

Home Sweet Home

This Australian homestead with its neat vegetable garden, windmill and water tank will delight anyone who has ever dreamt of owning a house in the country. The sampler was designed and stitched by Anne Boud.

PREPARATION

❖

Machine-zigzag or whip-stitch the edges of the fabric to prevent fraying. Find the centre of the fabric by folding it in half horizontally and then in half vertically. Stitch a running thread from side to side and top to bottom to mark the centre. Lightly mark the graph from arrow to arrow to correspond.

STITCHING

❖

Each Cross Stitch is represented by one square on the chart (see pattern sheet) which contains a symbol. These symbols refer to the DMC colours used in your embroidery. Refer to the key to the symbols before you start stitching.

Use three strands of cotton for Cross Stitch, but check the special instructions for Back Stitch. Start stitching from the centre of the design and work outwards. Leave the border until last.

To begin, hold the thread behind the fabric until a few stitches are worked over it to secure the loose end. Avoid using knots as these will result in a bump in your framed picture. To finish, weave the ends into the wrong side of the existing stitches so that they are anchored.

Do not carry a thread across the back of your work for more than four squares.

Each Cross Stitch is worked over one square of the material. Cross-stitch designs are usually worked from left to right, then right to left to complete the cross. In each cross, the top stitch must be worked in the same direction.

Work the design, personalising it with your chosen name and date.

SPECIAL INSTRUCTIONS

❖

Outlining in Back Stitch is done with two strands of cotton. For the chimney use 611; the veranda balustrade 501; the tank and tap 646; and the windmill 3787.

Centre the desired name and date and Back-stitch in 919. Use a Half Back Stitch or French Knot for the dots of 'i' and 'j'. Back-stitch the stems in the floral border using 520.

❖

MATERIALS

- 38cm x 42cm (15in x 16½in) 14-count ecru Aida

- DMC Stranded Embroidery Cotton: very dark shell pink (221), light shell pink (223), very light shell pink (224), very dark blue violet (333), very dark salmon (347), dark blue green (501), very dark fern green (520), dark drab brown (611), very dark beaver grey (645), medium beaver grey (647), very light tan (738), medium yellow (743), medium cornflower blue (793), medium garnet (815), very dark coral red (817), very dark beige brown (838), dark burnt orange (900), red copper (919), dark green grey (3051), green grey (3053), dark pine green (3362), medium pine green (3363), pine green (3364), dark beaver grey (646), dark brown grey (3787)

- No 26 tapestry needle

STITCHES USED

Cross Stitch, Back Stitch, French Knots

STITCH COUNT

128 wide x 147 high

FINISHED SIZE

23cm x 27cm (9in x 10½in)

Petit Point to Treasure

Here's proof of the saying that it's the little things that mean a lot. These finely stitched earrings, pendant and stick pin would be perfect to make for yourself or as a keepsake for a special friend.

KEY — Gumnuts Blossoms

1 = 054

2 = 052

3 = 051

4 = 050

5 = 645

6 = 644

7 = 643

8 = 675

9 = 674

10 = 991

X = CENTRE

VIVALDI ROSE POSY

EMBROIDERY DESIGN

(Actual Size)

Cross Stitch Silhouettes

This elegant lady and her gentleman companion are the epitome of Edwardian style. Their silhouette images were designed and stitched by Maxeen Cashion using Rajmahal Art Silk on ecru linen.

PREPARATION

Zigzag or bind the edges of the linen to prevent fraying. Find the centre of the fabric by folding it in half vertically and then working a running stitch top to bottom along the fold. Next, fold it horizontally and stitch as before. The stitching will intersect at the centre point of the fabric and correspond to the arrows shown on the graph on the pattern sheet.

STITCHING

Count from the centre of the fabric to the corresponding place on the graph you wish to start. Cross stitch is usually worked left to right and then right to left and these should all lie in the same direction. Do not use a thread longer than 45-50cm (18-20in) or it may wear thin, giving an uneven appearance. Separate your threads and then put them together again before threading the needle to help the stitches lie flat.

Start stitching by knotting the thread and coming through from the front of the work about 7cm (3in) to the left of where you intend to make your first Cross Stitch. After you have worked a few stitches, snip off the knot and thread the silk into the needle to weave it through the back of the stitches. When you wish to finish off a thread, weave the excess through the back of the stitches in the same way as with the starting thread.

Complete all the Cross Stitches and Half Cross Stitches before working the Back Stitching.

MATERIALS

- 55cm x 40cm (22in x 16in) 27-count ecru linen for each figure
- Rajmahal Art Silk: 2 skeins of No 25 for each figure
- Embroidery frame
- No 26 tapestry needle

STITCHES USED

Cross Stitch, Half Cross Stitch, Back Stitch

FINISHED SIZE

11cm x 27cm (4$\frac{1}{2}$in x 10$\frac{1}{2}$in)

NOTE: All stitches are worked with two strands of silk over two threads of the linen.

Ribbons and Roses Baby Blanket

For that very special baby, embroider a floral garland of gentle pastel roses, rosebuds, lavender, daisies and forget-me-nots entwined with lavender bows. Designed and stitched by Lee Lockheed, this delightful blanket is an excellent introduction to wool embroidery.

PREPARATION

Trace the position of the roses from the design outline on the pattern sheet onto the tracing paper. Centre the paper onto the blanket and make a hole in it with a needle at the centre of each rose. Then push the water-erasable pen through each hole to mark the position of the roses onto the blanket. It is not necessary to trace the other flowers as these can be added freehand once the roses have been stitched.

EMBROIDERY

The tapestry wool consists of four lightly twisted strands. The embroidery is worked entirely with the wool, carefully split into two strands. Work the flowers in the order given below.

Roses: Work four Colonial Knots using pink (7221) for the centre of each rose. Then with pale pink (7200), surround the Knots with three rows of Stem Stitch, worked closely together.

Daisies: Refering to the design for placement, work four Lazy Daisy Stitch petals for each daisy in ecru. Finish the daisies with a lemon (7905) Colonial-knot centre.

Forget-me-nots: The petals are five blue (7715) Colonial Knots with a lemon (7905) Colonial-knot centre.

Leaves: Each leaf consists of two small Straight Stitches worked side by side. The leaves are worked in pairs in the shape of a 'V'. Work the first leaf using green (7424) and the second leaf using pale green (7400).

Lavender knots: Using lavender (7722), work Colonial Knots close to each rose. The position of the lavender knots alternates; one group is worked on the inside and the next on the outside of each rose.

Bows: Stem-stitch the loops and tails of the bows using lavender (7722). Finish each bow with three Straight Stitches worked closely together for the centre knot.

Rosebuds: Use the pale green (7400) to work a Fly Stitch for the rosebud calyx. Fill each Fly Stitch with one Straight-stitch bud using the pale pink (7200).

Hail spots: With the water-erasable pen, draw a grid of straight lines 8cm (3in) apart along the length and across the width of the blanket to form a network of squares. Work small dots where the lines intersect and in the centre of each square. The dots are small Straight Stitches in pale pink (7200) worked five times over, into and out of the same holes

BACKING AND BINDING

Tack the lining fabric to the back of the blanket. Attach the binding to the edge of the blanket, mitring the corners. When the backing and binding are finished, work a line of Stem Stitch using pale pink (7200) on the blanketing, very close to the edge of the binding.

MATERIALS

- 72cm x 56cm (28³⁄₈in x 22in) wool blanketing
- 72cm x 56cm (28³⁄₈in x 22in) lining fabric (pre-shrunk)
- DMC Tapestry Wool: 1 skein each of pale pink (7200), pink (7221), pale green (7400), green (7424), blue (7715), lavender (7722), lemon (7905) and ecru
- 3.7m (4yd) lavender blanket binding
- No 20 tapestry needle
- Water-erasable pen
- Tracing paper

STITCHES USED

Colonial Knots, Stem Stitch, Lazy Daisy Stitch, Fly Stitch, Straight Stitch

FINISHED SIZE

72cm x 56cm (28³⁄₈in x 22in)

RIBBONS AND ROSES BABY BLANKET

DESIGN OUTLINE

(Actual Size)

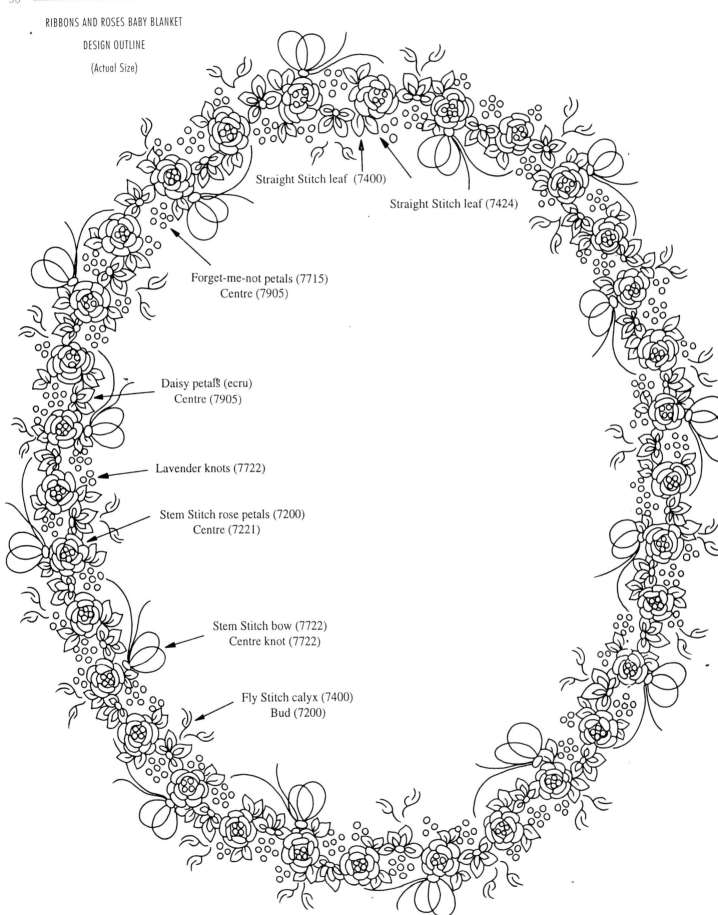

Straight Stitch leaf (7400)

Straight Stitch leaf (7424)

Forget-me-not petals (7715)
Centre (7905)

Daisy petals (ecru)
Centre (7905)

Lavender knots (7722)

Stem Stitch rose petals (7200)
Centre (7221)

Stem Stitch bow (7722)
Centre knot (7722)

Fly Stitch calyx (7400)
Bud (7200)

Christmas Bush Envelope Bag

Brazilian embroidery threads give this Australian wildflower design by Annette Rich a lustrous sheen. The natural shades of the Christmas Bush are captured by mixing plain and variegated colours.

MATERIALS

- 50cm (²/₃yd) square white Trigger cloth
- 50cm (²/₃yd) square Pellon
- 28cm x 18cm (11in x 7in) iron-on interfacing
- 50cm (²/₃yd) square cotton fabric for lining
- Edmar Rayon Threads: 1 skein each of Glory green/brown (45), light forest green (167), pink (153), light to pale olive green (49); 1 skein each of Iris green/brown (45), medium to light moss green (51), medium to light pink (4); 1 skein each of Lola medium pink (155), dark antique rose (163)
- Tissue paper
- Iron-on transfer pencil or IBC water-soluble fine tip pen
- 16cm (6¹/₄in) wooden embroidery hoop
- No 5 milliner's needle or No 7 straw needle
- No 3 darner needle
- Plain paper (for template)

STITCHES USED

Stem Stitch, Closed Fly Stitch, Straight Stitch, Lazy Daisy, French Knot, Long-legged Bullion Stitch

PREPARATION

❖

Cut a paper template of the envelope shape following the measurements on the pattern (page 80). When you are satisfied with the accuracy of your template, allow a 1cm (³/₈in) seam allowance all round and cut one from the Trigger cloth, one from the lining fabric and one from the Pellon.

Press over a 1cm (³/₈in) seam on all the edges of the Trigger cloth and the lining fabric and carefully and accurately press the folds as marked on the pattern. Press the iron-on interfacing to the front flap where you intend to embroider.

TRANSFERRING THE DESIGN

❖

Using an iron-on transfer pencil and tissue paper, trace the embroidery design. Centre the design on the front flap of the Trigger cloth and iron it on. You can use the water-soluble fine tip pen and transfer it, using the lightbox method.

It is not necessary to transfer the entire design, just mark as much as you need to work the embroidery, referring regularly to the design as you go.

HANDLING THE THREADS

❖

The Edmar Rayon threads need to be prepared and handled in a special way as follows:

Cut the tag off the skein and put it aside. Place the skein over the end of the ironing board and press it with a warm iron. Cut both sides of the little knot, through all the threads. Place the tag and the cut thread in a small plastic bag (if using a rayon thread keeper, follow the instructions supplied.

To decide which end to thread through the needle, rub the ends of the thread between your thumb and first finger. The end that frays the most is the end to thread through the needle. Dampen the end and thread the needle, trimming off the damp bit.

Begin work with a substantial knot and finish off firmly again with a knot.

Always use a frame with the fabric drum-tight. Stitching at times may be a stabbing-stitch motion, rather than a sewing motion.

At regular intervals, turn the work upside down and hang the needle and thread down to allow the thread to unwind.

When making Bullions, always wind the thread clockwise onto the needle.

EMBROIDERY

❖

Use a No 5 milliner's needle for the Iris thread and Glory and No 3 darner for Lola.

Work the main branches first using the brown portion of the green/brown Iris (45). The small stems are worked with the green/brown Glory (45), taking advantage of the colour changes for a natural shading effect. Embroider both in Stem Stitch.

Work the larger leaves in medium to light moss green Iris (51). Work the small leaves in light forest green Glory (167). Both are stitched in Closed Fly Stitch (refer to the stitch diagram).

Work the little leaves and some of the little stems also in light forest green Glory (167), using Stem Stitch and eight-wrap Bullions for the little leaves.

The petal centres are small Straight Stitches in medium pink (155) and dark antique rose Lola (163). Spread the two shades all over the design, with more dark thread at the bottom and more pale at the top.

Work a Lazy Daisy Stitch in pink Glory (153) around each Straight Stitch but don't pull this stitch too tight. Finish the flowers with a single or double wrap French Knot in light to pale olive green Glory (49) in the centre.

LAUNDERING

❖

When the embroidery is finished, wash it carefully. Use fairly hot water with a little washing liquid and sprinkle salt on the embroidered area before placing it in the water. Soak it for five minutes or so to remove any transfer marks, then rinse it well under cold running water. Rinse it again in warm water with a good dash of white vinegar and salt, then rinse it yet again in plain cold water.

Hang it to dry out of direct sunlight and, when dry, place it face down on a well-padded ironing board and press it, carefully re-ironing the fold lines.

MAKING UP

❖

Place the embroidered piece on a table, right side facing you and the bottom corner nearest to you. Cover it with the lining, right side down, and place the Pellon onto the wrong side of the lining.

Machine-sew around all the edges leaving a 12.5cm (5cm) opening on one flap edge. Trim the seams and cut away any excess Pellon, snipping across the corners.

Turn it to the right side through the opening, flatten all the seams and push out the corners well. Press the opening seam allowance under and invisibly hand-stitch closed. Press it again, then press the bottom and side flaps into the middle along the fold lines. Invisibly hand-stitch these flaps to each other along the seams. Then fold down the top flap and press it again.

To finish the bag, work 10 to 15-wrap Long-legged Bullions with medium to light pink Iris (4) on the seams and along the top edge of the flap (see the stitch diagram). ✿

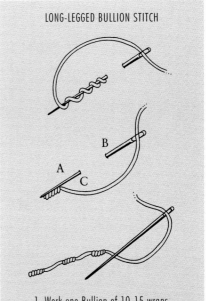

LONG-LEGGED BULLION STITCH

1. Work one Bullion of 10-15 wraps.

2. After working Bullion A, do not take the needle and thread to the back of fabric, but move it to point B (about twice the length of the first Bullion). Go through the fabric at B and come back through at C. Work another Bullion.

3. Continue in this manner until the desired number of Bullions have been worked.

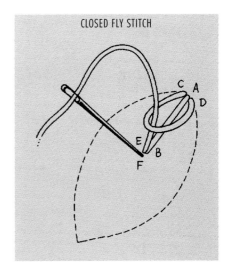

CLOSED FLY STITCH

Blue and White Rose

This rose by Erica Wilson, one of America's foremost needlepoint designers, was adapted from the pattern on centuries-old blue and white porcelain in the collection of the Metropolitan Museum of Modern Art in New York. Bette Doulis of Priscilla's Tapestry stitched the design in Paternayan wool against a background of lustrous Perlé Cotton.

PREPARATION

❖

Fold the canvas into four sections to find the centre position. Using the tapestry needle and some spare thread, stitch across and down in small even tacking stitches to mark the middle of the canvas.

Using these tacking lines, measure out from the centre and mark a rectangle 26cm x 16.5cm (10in x 6½in) with a running stitch using one strand of wool. It is recommended that you tack the outline of the rectangle and not mark it in pencil, to avoid getting graphite marks on the Perlé thread. This is the size of the completed design.

Next, Back-stitch the canvas securely onto the frame and tighten the end screws to give a firm base for stitching.

STITCHING

❖

Find the centre stitch on the graph on the pattern (page 78) and start stitching from that point using Continental Stitch, remembering that each square on the graph represents one stitch on the canvas.

To begin stitching, use the No 20 tapestry needle and two strands of Paternayan wool. Thread the needle and put a knot in the end, then go down from the front through the canvas about 2.5cm (1in) away from your starting point. As you stitch you will then cover the thread which lies on the back of your work, and when you reach the knot you can simply cut it off. This starting method is called a waste knot.

Use a 'stabbing' technique to your stitch rather than a 'sewing' method.

To finish off your thread, run it through some stitches on the back of your work, then snip it off.

Continue stitching, working in Continental Stitch for all the blue outlines. For stitching the unmarked areas, use white Perlé No 3, Continental Stitch, and the No 20 tapestry needle. The Perlé cotton should be approximately 30cm (12in) in length.

Remove the tacking stitches before commencing the Basket Weave, stitching the background outside the rose in white Perlé.

FINISHING

❖

When all the background stitching has been completed, hold your work up to the light to see if you have missed any stitches. Make any necessary adjustments before removing your work from the tapestry frame. You can then take your work to be professionally blocked and framed, or finish it whichever way you prefer. ❀

MATERIALS

- 30cm x 38cm (12in x 15in) 14-count Mono canvas
- No 20 and 28 tapestry needles
- Paternayan wool: 1 skein each of dark blue (510), mid blue (501), light blue (552)
- DMC Perlé Cotton No 3: 7 skeins in white
- 38cm (15in) tapestry lap frame
- Ruler
- Embroidery scissors
- Needle and thread for stitching canvas to frame

STITCHES USED

Continental Stitch, Basket Weave Stitch

FINISHED SIZE

26cm x 16.5cm (10¼in x 6½in)

Gone Fishin'

If you've ever wondered what a bear does on his day off, now you know. Jenny Bradford designed and stitched this charming picture as a companion piece to one found in her book, Jenny Bradford's Designs for Teddy Bears.

PREPARATION

Photocopy or trace the pattern and place the fabric over it using the water-soluble pen to trace the outline of the bear, the river bank outline and any other areas of the design, such as bulrushes, fishing line and fish.

Do not mark the fabric with the exact position of all the flowers and greenery as this is intended to be a free design, offering an opportunity for your own creativity.

If you wish, back the fabric with a lightweight interfacing.

Next, put the traced fabric into an embroidery frame.

EMBROIDERY

Single threads of stranded cotton have been used throughout unless otherwise specified. The bear is embroidered in Long and Short Stitch using a single strand of thread to simulate fur. Care should be taken to work the stitching in the right direction. Mix colours gold (783) and dark gold (781) to fill in the main body parts. Work with dark gold (781) only where heavier shadow is required, for example around the muzzle and along the gusset lines on the face, on the body below the arm, on the leg and ankle crease, and around the foot pad. Work the muzzle in pale gold (677), radiating stitches out from the nose area. The inner ear and paw pads are worked in Satin Stitch, using the same thread.

Use two strands of black to work a single Colonial Knot for each eye.

Highlight the eyes with a tiny Straight Stitch in white. Satin-stitch the nose and work the mouth in Straight Stitch with a single strand of black thread. Work the outline of the river bank in Stem Stitch

using two strands of DMC medium butterscotch (3828).

Scatter small Straight Stitches to simulate grass, filling in the area between the river bank and the bear. Continue to stitch along the line of the river bank reducing the size of the stitches as it recedes into the distance.

Work the bulrushes as follows: Using Minnamurra green variegated (250), work the leaves as closely placed rows of Stem Stitch and the flower stems in single Straight Stitches with two strands. Bulrush heads are worked in YLI Silk Floss camel (83), using three strands for these in the foreground and two for those in the background. Work a single Straight Stitch of the required length for the centre of the head, then work two slightly shorter Straight Stitches on each side of the centre stitch. Work a small Straight Stitch at the top of the bulrush head.

Work gold grasses in Straight Stitch using three strands of YLI Silk Floss gold beige (181) for the grass in the foreground, and two strands and smaller stitches for the clusters in the background.

Using a single strand of Minnamurra green variegated (250), work French

MATERIALS

- 28cm x 22cm (11in x 8⅝in) homespun or similar (backed with lightweight interfacing if required)

- Minnamurra Stranded Cotton: 1 skein each of green variegated (250), purple variegated (10)

- DMC Stranded Embroidery Cotton: 1 skein each of pale gold (677), gold (783), dark gold (781), green (522), medium butterscotch (3828), light brown (840), black, white

- DMC Perlé Cotton No 5: light brown (840)

- YLI Silk Floss: 1 skein each of camel (83), gold beige (181), red (4), aqua (046)

- Fine metallic thread or machine-embroidery thread in silver grey

- No 9 crewel needle

- Bird charm (fish charm optional)

- Water-soluble fine line marker

- Embroidery frame

STITCHES USED

Long and Short Stitch, Satin Stitch, Colonial Knot, Straight Stitch, Stem Stitch, French Knot, Back Stitch, Fly Stitch, Uneven Lazy Daisy Stitch, Couching Stitch

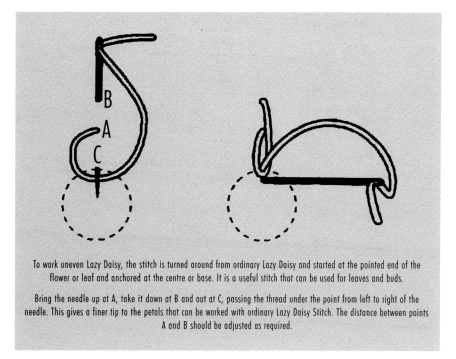

To work uneven Lazy Daisy, the stitch is turned around from ordinary Lazy Daisy and started at the pointed end of the flower or leaf and anchored at the centre or base. It is a useful stitch that can be used for leaves and buds.

Bring the needle up at A, take it down at B and out at C, passing the thread under the point from left to right of the needle. This gives a finer tip to the petals that can be worked with ordinary Lazy Daisy Stitch. The distance between points A and B should be adjusted as required.

Knots of greenery in the background and Colonial Knots for the foreground along the edge of the bank at the bear's feet. Using two strands of YLI Silk Floss red (4), scatter knots through the greenery.

Work the daisies in Uneven Lazy Daisy Stitch (see diagram), using Minnamurra purple variegated (10) over the grass stitches in the foreground. Add the leaves also in Uneven Lazy Daisy Stitch. Work Colonial Knots to add a hint of colour to the area beyond the bear's foot.

Using YLI Silk Floss aqua (046), work long Straight Stitches to represent the ripples on the water.

Couch a single thread of Perlé No 5 light brown (840) in place with a single strand of matching stranded cotton for the fishing rod. Work one long Straight Stitch in machine-embroidery thread to represent the fishing line.

If you choose to embroider the fish, Back-stitch the outline with very small stitches in machine-embroidery or fine metallic thread. Fill in the fins with Straight Stitches and fill in the body with tiny Fly Stitches to form a diamond pattern. Work the eye with a French Knot in one strand of black silk or cotton.

FINISHING

❖

Remove any design marks with a wet cotton bud or wash the embroidery carefully. Sew the bird and fish charms in position as required.

Your bear picture is now complete and ready for framing.

Phoebe's Jumper

Leisa Pownall has transformed this inexpensive store-bought jumper into a beautiful one-off fashion garment. Her Bullion Loop roses, daisies and Feather Stitch can be adapted to suit many designs.

PREPARATION

Tack the interfacing to the wrong side of the jumper, making sure it covers the entire area to be embroidered. This stabilises the jumper and makes it easier to embroider.

EMBROIDERY

Work the large roses first, in the centre of a pattern on the jumper. Add the daisies around another pattern, not necessarily in a diamond shape, and join them with the Feather Stitch in light green (1408). Use your imagination to adapt the design to suit the pattern on your jumper.

The Bullion Loop roses are worked in six strands of floss. Start with a knot on the end of the thread (see the step-by-step photograph). Do three, 18-wrap Bullion Loops in purple (0903), worked closely together. In the same colour, work a two-wrap French Knot in the centre.

In the medium cornflower blue (0902), work five, 18-wrap Bullion Loop petals surrounding the first three. Make sure they sit in the gaps between the petals and not directly behind them.

In the cornflower blue (0901), work seven, 20-wrap Bullion Loop petals around the previous five. Again, make sure that the loops sit between the petals of the previous round.

In green (1603), put eight to nine, 20-wrap Bullion Loops around the previous round. The green petals are not as closely spaced as the first three rounds.

Embroider the daisies next in Lazy Daisy Stitch using six strands of yellow (0113) floss. These have five petals, the first three worked in a 'Y' shape. The fourth and fifth petals will fit perfectly between petals 1 and 3 and 2 and 3 (see the step-by step photograph). Finish

MATERIALS

- Jumper in cotton or wool

- Medium to heavyweight interfacing (enough to cover the jumper front)

- No 3 milliner's (straw) needle

- Madeira embroidery floss: two packets each of green (1603), cornflower blue (0901), yellow (0113); one packet each of light green (1408), medium cornflower blue (0902), purple (0903)

- Madeira four strand metallic thread 9805 blackgold (5014)

- Lawn or flannelette for lining back of work (optional)

STITCHES USED

Bullion Stitch, Chain Stitch, Colonial Knot, French Knot, Lazy Daisy, Feather Stitch

with a Colonial Knot in four strands of metallic thread at the centre of the daisy.

After you have embroidered all the daisies in the diamond shape (or whatever shape your jumper dictates), join them with Feather Stitch using two strands of light green (1408). Make sure all the Feather Stitches go in the same direction, so that the left side is worked separately from the right side.

FINISHING

When all the embroidery has been finished, cut away the excess interfacing. If you wish, you can line the back of your work. Cut a piece of lining the same shape as the jumper front, but allow for a 1cm (³⁄₈in) hem all around. Iron the hem down and slip-stitch the lining to

the back of your work. You now have a beautiful and unique jumper worth far more than you paid for the original. ✿

Needle Threader Pendant

*Subtly-shaded graduated ribbon gives a delicate beauty to this
practical pendant, designed and stitched by Jenny Bradford.
Not only is it a pretty thing you'll love to wear, but you'll always know
where your favourite needle threader is.*

MATERIALS

- 12cm x 20cm (4³/₄in x 8in) Jobelan or similar evenweave fabric
- 20cm (8in) square Soft-Sew Vilene
- 7mm (¹/₄in) Fancyworks graduated silk ribbon: 4m (4³/₈yd) Colour No 3 for pendant with old rose tassel or Colour No 8 for pendant with blue tassel
- Gumnut Silk Buds: one skein of old rose (867) or blue (406) for each tassel
- Mill Hill petite beads: gold (42011) or pearl (40123)
- 12cm x 6cm (4³/₄in x 2¹/₂in) template plastic or card for each pendant
- Needle threader in gold or silver
- No 24 tapestry needle
- No 18 chenille needle
- Nymo thread for sewing beads
- Sewing thread to match even-weave fabric
- 7cm (2³/₄in) embroidery hoop
- Small screwdriver (or similar implement)

STITCHES USED

Looped Straight Stitch, Ribbon Stitch, Blanket Stitch, Palestrina Knot Stitch, Whip Stitch

PREPARATION

Cut two, 5.5cm (2¹/₄in) diameter circles from cardboard or template plastic. Back the fabric with Soft-Sew Vilene, tacking together around the edges. Mark two circles on the reverse side of the fabric with one template, leaving 3cm (1¹/₄in) between the circles and around the outer edges.

Using small stitches and matching thread, tack around the outline of each circle.

STITCHING

The ribbon embroidery is worked with the No 18 chenille needle.

Centre one circle in the embroidery hoop and draw a 3mm (¹/₈in) diameter circle for the centre of each flower, as shown in the diagram (page 54).

Work the flower petals in Looped Straight Stitch by coming up on the edge of the marked centre and taking the needle to the back of the work, directly in line with the first point and 2-3mm (¹/₈in) outside the edge of the marked circle. Take care to spread the ribbon and work without twists. Pull the ribbon through carefully, leaving a loop of about 8mm (³/₈in) on the surface. As each successive loop is made, care must be taken not to shorten the previous loops as they will be unstable until the centres of the flowers are worked. Work five or six petals around the marked circle for each flower.

Sew on petite beads for the flower centres, making sure that each petal is securely held in place at its base by the beads. If required, the angle of the petals can be adjusted slightly during this process.

Add leaves in Ribbon Stitch as shown in the diagram (page 54).

The green section of the graduated ribbon should be used for the leaves.

FINISHING

Trim the Soft-Sew Vilene back to the circle tacking line on both pieces and cut two extra Soft-Sew Vilene discs to cover one template.

Cut out the fabric circles with a 1.5cm (⁵/₈in) seam allowance. Using strong thread, run a gathering thread 1cm (³/₈in) from the cut edge of each circle.

Place the embroidered circle face down and centre on it the two extra Soft-Sew Vilene circles and the template disc. Pull up the gathering thread to secure the embroidery around the template.

Cover the second template in the same way, using the plain circle of fabric without the extra padding.

To make the twisted cord, cut two, 2.25m (2¹/₂yd) two-strand lengths from the skein of Silk Buds. Thread both lengths through the top of the needle threader and position it in the centre of the threads. Pin the threader securely to a pillow or padded ironing board so that you can tighten the threads as you work.

Take four strands in each hand and roll the threads held in the right hand to the right (clockwise). Pass these threads to the left hand over the threads already held in the left hand which are then passed to the right hand. Keep repeating the process of rolling and passing from hand to hand. With a little practice it is easy to work a very evenly twisted cord using the following hints:

- Dampen the fingers to roll the threads easily and keep a firm tension as you work. This cord does not unravel if you let go but, if you do let go, re-tension the last few wraps by pulling the two sets of threads slightly apart before resuming the twisting process.

- Knot the threads together at the end of the cord.

Fold the cord in half and up the centre of the wrong side of the plain-covered disc. The knotted end of the cord and the threader should lie at the bottom, and the looped end should lie at the top. Place the embroidered disc (right side up) over the plain disc and cord. Ladder-stitch the two discs together but do not sew through the cords; they should slide freely through the centre of the pendant.

Cut two, 75cm (30in) lengths of Silk Buds thread for working Palestrina Knot. Stitch around the outer edge of the pendant. Using the tapestry needle and a two-strand length of thread, work Palestrina Knot Stitch, picking up two or three threads of fabric at the edge of each disc as you work the small vertical stitch. Keep the stitches close to form a neat corded edge and work through the front disc only as you pass over the twisted cords.

Make a tassel from the remaining silk thread. Cut a single strand 1.8m (2yd) long for embroidering the tassel head. Set aside. Wind the remainder around a small piece of card 6.5cm (2¹/₂in) wide. Tie the loops at the top of the tassel before cutting through the wraps and removing the tassel from the card.

Tie one end of the thread you have set aside around the neck of the tassel, one-third of the way down from the top. Wind the thread twice around the tassel and tie firmly with a flat knot.

Thread the tapestry needle with the long end of the thread, turn the tassel, hold it so that the top end is pointing towards you and work a row of Blanket Stitch over the neck tie. Do not pull the Blanket Stitches too tightly as you will work the next row into these, as shown in the diagram.

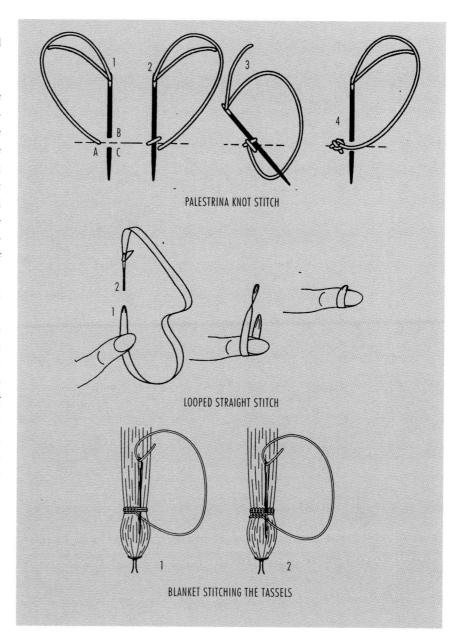

PALESTRINA KNOT STITCH

LOOPED STRAIGHT STITCH

BLANKET STITCHING THE TASSELS

Take care not to work into the actual threads of the tassel head.

Keep working rows of Blanket Stitch until two-thirds of the tassel head are covered, then Whip-stitch into each stitch of the last row.

Using a small screwdriver, push the remaining part of the tassel head and the knotted end of the twisted cord inside the stitched heading before pulling the heading tightly around the stuffing and sewing off securely. Pass the needle down through the tassel head

and trim the thread end level with the tassel threads. Repeat with the other thread ends.

Finish the tassel by trimming the bottom evenly and sewing beads around the neck as desired.

Slide the needle threader into the gap between the embroidered flowers, adjusting the length of the cord as required.

A Perfect Pair

*The delicate shades of hand-dyed silk contrast beautifully
with the dramatic black velvet background in this
ribbon embroidery by Bev Gogel.*

MATERIALS

PINK AND IVORY ROSES

- 35cm (14in) square of black cotton velvet or fabric of your choice
- Handpainted bread dough vase
- Petals 7mm (¹/₄in) hand-dyed silk ribbon: 2.75m (3yd) each of copper rose, brown sugar
- Petals 4mm (¹/₈in) hand-dyed silk ribbon: 2.75m (3yd) of brown sugar
- YLI 7mm (¹/₄in) silk ribbon: 1m (1¹/₈yd) antique green (56)
- YLI 4mm (1/8in) silk ribbon: 1m (1¹/₈yd) antique green (56)
- Madeira stranded cotton: one skein each of olive green (1606), honey (2207), pale honey (2205)
- Minnamurra MT160
- Machine or embroidery thread to match the Petals ribbons
- No 1 and 7 milliner's (straw) needles
- No 20 chenille needle
- Craft glue
- Blu-Tack

HONEY ROSE BOUQUET

- 35cm (14in) square of black cotton velvet or fabric of your choice
- Handpainted bread dough urn
- Petals 7mm (¹/₄in) hand-dyed silk ribbon: 2.75m (3yd) each of brown sugar, burnt almond
- Petals 4mm (¹/₄in) hand-dyed silk ribbon: 2.75m (3yd) brown sugar
- YLI 7mm (¹/₄in) silk ribbon: 1m (1¹/₈yd) antique green (6)
- YLI 4mm (¹/₈in) silk ribbon: 1m (1¹/₈yd) antique green (56)
- Machine or embroidery thread to match the Petals ribbons
- No 1 and No 7 milliner's (straw) needles
- No 20 chenille needle
- Craft glue
- Blu-Tack

STITCHES USED

Folded Ribbon Rose, Ribbon Stitch, Looped Straight Stitch, Straight Stitch, Stem Stitch, Bullion Stitch, French Knots

FINISHED SIZE

9cm (3¹/₂in) square (approximately)

PREPARATION

Overlock the edges of the fabric to avoid fraying. Position the bottom of the vase in the centre of the fabric, approximately 9cm (3¹/₂in) from the lower edge, and Blu-Tack into place. The vase should be glued to the fabric only once the embroidery has been completed and the fabric has been stretched for framing. Follow the same procedure for the urn.

EMBROIDERY

Pink and Ivory Roses

Refer to the design outline and diagram 2 to make the folded ribbon roses.

Roses: Using the No 1 Milliner's needle and two strands of matching thread, make four ribbon roses of approximately 12mm (¹/₂in) in diameter with Petals 7mm (¹/₄in) copper rose ribbon, then three roses of a similar size in Petals 7mm brown sugar ribbon.

Following the design outline, nestle the ribbon roses into position and stitch gently in place. Work pairs of Looped Straight Stitches between the roses and between the bouquet and the top edge of the vase, using YLI 4mm (¹/₈in) antique green silk ribbon. This is simply a loop of ribbon, worked in and out of the same hole, which sits on the surface of the fabric. Care must be taken that the ribbon does not twist or pull through. A knitting needle or pencil slipped into the loop will ensure all loops are the same size.

Refer to the colour and stitch key for the positions of the outer foliage to complete the arrangement.

Bullions: With six strands of thread and the milliner's needle, work Bullions of approximately 18 wraps, using the colours indicated on the design outline.

Leaves: Stitch the leaves using your chenille needle and YLI 7mm (¹/₄in) antique green ribbon. The larger leaves are single Ribbon Stitches and the smaller leaves are worked in Straight Stitches.

Buds and silk ribbon French Knots: Using the chenille needle, work the rosebuds with Straight Stitches. Graduate the bud size from larger to smaller, working from the centre of the design to the outer edge of the stem to give the bouquet a natural flow. Use Petals 7mm (¹/₄in) brown sugar ribbon for the buds and French Knots from the brown sugar rose centres. Use the Petals 7mm (¹/₄in) copper rose ribbon for the large buds and French Knots to the right, and Petals 7mm (¹/₄in) brown sugar ribbon for the large buds to the left and the top. The outermost buds are worked using Petals 4mm (¹/₈in) brown sugar silk ribbon.

Calyx and stems: Using the straw needle and blending one strand of Madeira olive green (1606) together with one strand of honey (2207), work a small stitch to form the calyx of each Straight-stitch petal, Bullion and French Knot. Bring the thread up at the base of the petal, Bullion or French Knot, then take the thread under the petal and through the loop of thread (diagram 1). Pull the thread firmly to form a small, neat knot. The holding stitch of the knot becomes the Straight-stitch stem, joining the buds, leaves and Bullions as shown in the design outline. Work these stitches loosely to give your work curvature and flow.

Honey Rose Bouquet

Refer to the design outline.

Roses: Using the No 7 Milliner's needle and two strands of matching thread, make three ribbon roses of approximately 12mm (¹/₂in) in diameter with Petals 7mm (¹/₄in) brown sugar

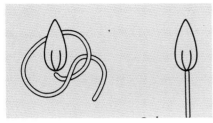

Diagram 1 – Calyx

ribbon, then three roses of a similar size in Petals 7mm (¹⁄₄in) burnt almond ribbon.

Following the design outline, nestle the roses into position and stitch gently in place. Work pairs of Looped Straight Stitches between the roses and between the bouquet and the top edge of the urn using YLI 4mm (¹⁄₈in) antique green silk ribbon. Add the outer foliage to the arrangement.

Bullions: With six strands of thread and the milliner's needle, work Bullions of approximately 18 wraps, using the colours indicated on the design outline.

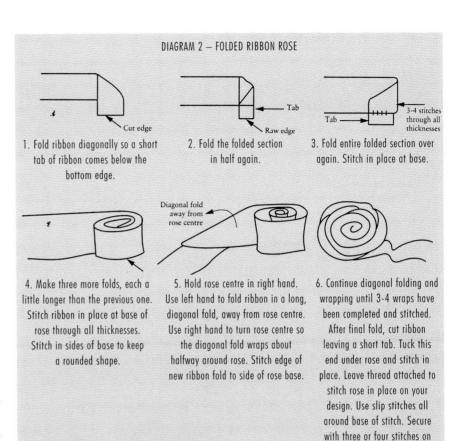

DIAGRAM 2 — FOLDED RIBBON ROSE

1. Fold ribbon diagonally so a short tab of ribbon comes below the bottom edge. *Cut edge*

2. Fold the folded section in half again. *Tab* *Raw edge*

3. Fold entire folded section over again. Stitch in place at base. *Tab* *3-4 stitches through all thicknesses*

4. Make three more folds, each a little longer than the previous one. Stitch ribbon in place at base of rose through all thicknesses. Stitch in sides of base to keep a rounded shape.

5. Hold rose centre in right hand. Use left hand to fold ribbon in a long, diagonal fold, away from rose centre. Use right hand to turn rose centre so the diagonal fold wraps about halfway around rose. Stitch edge of new ribbon fold to side of rose base. *Diagonal fold away from rose centre*

6. Continue diagonal folding and wrapping until 3-4 wraps have been completed and stitched. After final fold, cut ribbon leaving a short tab. Tuck this end under rose and stitch in place. Leave thread attached to stitch rose in place on your design. Use slip stitches all around base of stitch. Secure with three or four stitches on wrong side.

Leaves: Use the chenille needle and YLI 7mm (¹/₄in) antique green ribbon for the leaves. The larger leaves are single Ribbon Stitches and the smaller leaves are Straight Stitches.

Buds and silk ribbon French Knots: Using the chenille needle, work the rosebuds with Straight Stitches. Graduate the bud size from larger to smaller, working from the centre of the design to the outer edge of the stem to give the bouquet a natural flow. Use Petals 7mm (¹/₄in) brown sugar ribbon for the buds and French Knots radiating from the brown sugar rose centres. Use Petals 7mm (¹/₄in) burnt almond ribbon for the buds and French Knots that radiate from the burnt almond centre roses. The outermost buds are all worked using Petals 4mm (¹/₈in) brown sugar silk ribbon.

Calyx and stems: Work as for Pink and Ivory Roses.

MAKING UP

❖

After stretching and lacing the velvet to the backing board, glue the vase permanently into place. Do the same with the urn. Take your work to a professional framer when complete – it should be placed in a box frame to allow space for the roses, and glass should be used to protect the embroidery from dust. ❀

HINT: When creating Bullion Stitches, use colours randomly throughout the design.

COLOUR KEY

1 = Petals copper rose

2 = Petals brown sugar

Minnamurra MT160

Madeira pale honey 2205

Madeira honey 2207

STITCH KEY

Leaf

Bud

French Knots

DESIGN OUTLINE – PINK AND IVORY ROSES (Actual Size)

COLOUR KEY

1 = Petals brown sugar

2 = Petals brown almond

2207

2205

STITCH KEY

Leaf

Bud

French Knots

DESIGN OUTLINE – HONEY ROSE BOUQUET (Actual Size)

Hardanger Heart

The lustre of silk threads gives a touch of luxury to this dainty
heart design created by Emie Bishop for Kreinik threads.
Its small scale makes it perfect for the lid of a keepsake box.
It could also make a pretty pin or brooch cushion.

MATERIALS

- 20cm (8in) square 28-count Cashel linen in antique white

- Kreinik Silk Mori thread: one skein each of very dark mauve (1107), lightest wood violet (1092), medium dark mauve (1105),

- Kreinik Silk Serica thread: one skein each of lightest wood violet (1092), medium dark mauve (1105), very pale coral (3011), cream (7124), medium Victorian sheen (4164), very dark Victorian sheen (4167)

- No 24 tapestry needle

- Sharp fine-bladed embroidery scissors

- Embroidery hoop

- Pencil, ruler

STITCHES USED

Corner Dove's Eye, Rice Stitch, Woven Bars, Satin Stitch, Bullion Stitch, Cross Stitch

FINISHED SIZE

10cm (3⅞in) square

PREPARATION

Hand or machine-overcast the raw edges of the fabric to prevent unravelling. Fold the fabric in half horizontally and vertically and finger-press the folds. Following the warp and weft threads, run a line of basting stitches along the folds to mark the centre of the fabric.

Small arrows mark the centres of each side on the pattern. With a pencil and ruler, join these arrows side to side and top to bottom. These lines will correspond with the basting stitches.

Note: Each square on the graph represents two fabric threads on the stitch diagrams, and one line equals one thread. The Serica thread is not split. When using Mori thread, split into three strands, separate the strands and allow to untwist before rejoining.

EMBROIDERY

Commence with the central Satin-stitched heart design. Refer to diagram 1, noting that when the stitches turn a corner the hole is shared – the diagonal thread is not carried across the corner. Work the inner row of Satin Stitch (Klosters) in Serica lightest wood violet (1092), then the outer row in Serica medium dark mauve (1105).

Fill the space between Klosters with Rice Stitch (diagram 2) in Serica lightest wood violet (1092) for the bottom crosses. Work the top crosses in Serica medium dark mauve (1105).

Cut and remove the marked fabric threads from the inner portion of the heart (diagram 3). Remember one square on the graph equals two fabric threads, so you will be removing four threads and leaving four threads.

Following the graph, first cut the vertical threads as marked, by sliding the blade of your scissors under the four threads to be cut, and cutting as close as possible to the Satin Stitch. Go slowly and carefully, checking that you have the correct threads on the blade before cutting them. Cut a group of four threads, then cut the opposite end of the same four threads. Remove the threads gently by lifting them with a tapestry needle. Cut and remove the horizontal threads in the same way.

When all the threads have been removed, it is time to work the Woven Bars and Corner Dove's Eyes using Serica cream (7124).

Secure the thread under the Klosters and, referring to diagram 4, work in a figure eight motion under two fabric threads and over two. Use a tight tension and continue until the bar is full. Work all four bars and then work the Corner Dove's Eye (diagram 5). Move to the next bar to be woven and bring the

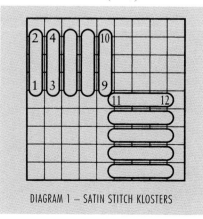

DIAGRAM 1 – SATIN STITCH KLOSTERS

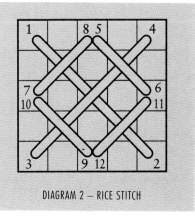

DIAGRAM 2 – RICE STITCH

KEY: Kreinik Silk Mori Thread ◫ 1092   ⊞ 1105   ♥♥ 1107   Kreinik Silk Serica Thread ⠿ 3011   ⊠ 4164   ⊞ 4167   ◫ 1092

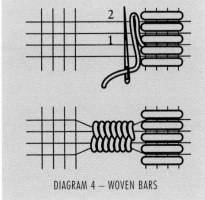

DIAGRAM 3 — CUTTING FABRIC THREADS

DIAGRAM 4 — WOVEN BARS

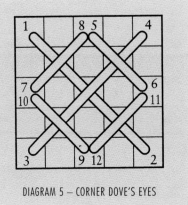

DIAGRAM 5 — CORNER DOVE'S EYES

needle up in the centre of the four threads. Complete all Cross Stitches using three strands of Mori, following the graph and key.

In each corner, work a Bullion Stitch using three strands of Mori in very dark mauve (1107).

Finally, Satin-stitch the outer border. The hearts are stitched in Serica medium dark mauve (1105). The tulip corners are stitched in Serica lightest wood violet (1092) and the scrolls in Serica very pale coral (3011).

Your Hardanger Heart is now finished and ready to be framed, made into a brooch cushion or inserted into a box lid.

Geraldton Wax Sampler

Brazilian embroidery techniques and lustrous rayon threads have been used by Annette Rich to capture the beauty of one of Australia's best-loved wildflowers, Geraldton Wax. Each of the five sprays is worked in a different colour scheme, ranging from soft pinks and mauves to rich purples.

MATERIALS

- 38cm x 46cm (15in x 18in) Australian Trigger Cloth

- Edmar Glory rayon thread: one skein each of medium to light rose (6), pink and violet (17), medium to light gold yellow (69), green and brown (45), medium to light avocado (50), dark to light plum (94), dark to light forest green (110)

- Edmar Iris rayon thread: one skein each of medium to light moss green (24), green and brown (45), medium to light avocado 50), medium to light plum (107), medium brown (120), pink and violet (17), lavender (125)

- No 7 straw needle or No 5 milliner's needle

- No 7 long darner

- IBC blue fine tip water-erasable felt transfer pen

- Tissue paper (or lunch wrap paper)

- Needle threader (optional)

- 10cm (4in) wooden embroidery hoop

- Rayon thread keeper (optional)

- White tape

STITCHES USED

Detached Chain (Lazy Daisy) Stitch, Satin Stitch, Bullion Stitch, Spider's Web, Stem Stitch, French Knot, Couching, Straight Stitch

FINISHED SIZE

23cm x 15cm (9in x 6in)

PREPARATION

❖

Using tissue paper and a normal pencil or felt tip pen, make a master design, arranging the sprays as a sampler or as you wish.

Centre the fabric over the master design and, using the IBC fine tip transfer pen, trace the design (page 83) carefully onto the fabric. It is not necessary to trace the entire design – only as much as you need to work the embroidery, referring regularly to the design and colour photograph as you stitch.

The inner ring of your embroidery hoop should be bound with white tape, and the fabric should be drum tight when in the hoop.

HANDLING THE THREADS

❖

Read through this section completely before proceeding.

Edmar rayon threads need to be prepared and handled differently from the usual embroidery thread. These tips will come in handy.

Remove the numbered tag from the skein and put safely aside. Place the skein over the end of your ironing board and press with a warm iron. Cut through all threads, both sides of the knot. Place both tag and thread in a thread keeper, following the instructions supplied. Alternatively, place the tag and thread in a small plastic bag. The threads are springy and need to be kept organised.

To decide which end to thread through the needle, rub the ends of the thread between your thumb and first finger. The end that frays the most is the end to thread through the needle. If you are not using a needle threader, dampen the end and thread the needle, then trim off the damp portion. Always begin your work with a substantial knot and finish off firmly.

Regularly turn your work upside down and hang the needle and thread down to unwind, running your fingers gently down the thread and over the needle.

Note: It is most important when making Bullions to wind the thread clockwise onto the needle.

The rayon threads are washable, even boilable. In this design, Annette recommends you pre-wash the dark to light plum (94). Remove the tag and keep to one side. Place the uncut skein in boiling salted water and boil for about 10 minutes. Rinse well under cold running water. Squeeze out the skein in a towel and leave to dry. When dry, straighten out the skein and press gently.

STITCHING

❖

The directions are given for design A. All the other sprays are worked using the same method, although the colours vary. See the table on page 66 for colours, needles and stitches.

Design A – Petals: Pad each petal with Detached Chain Stitch using the

SPIDER'S WEB

Work five Straight Stitches, like the spokes of a wheel. Bring the needle and thread up at the centre, then weave over and under the spokes until the area is filled. Finish off on the wrong side.

thread specified. Keeping a careful eye on the shape, work over this in Satin Stitch.

Make a large Bullion Stitch to wrap from one side of the petal around to the other. The number of times you wrap the thread will vary according to the size of the petal. As a general rule, do 40 or so wraps if using Iris; and 50 or so wraps if using Glory. Using the same thread, Couch down the long Bullions to shape them around the petals. The Couching Stitch should be as close to the Bullion as possible.

Centres: Using the colour specified, make five small Straight Stitches (like the spokes of a wheel) from the exact centre of the flower, pointing each to the base of a petal. Weave over and under these spokes, creating a Spider's Web.

Using Glory, make tiny overlapping Stem Stitches around the outer edge of the Spider's Web, leaving each stitch slightly loose. Work a two or three-wrap French Knot right in the centre of the Spider's Web.

On designs D and E, the centres each have a 30-wrap Bullion in Glory worked around each half of the centre. These are couched down.

Buds: Most buds are in Satin Stitch, worked in the same thread as specified for the petals. Add a green French Knot at the base for the calyx.

On designs D and E there are three bigger buds. Over the Satin Stitch, work a 20-wrap Bullion from the base of the bud towards the top. Catch this Bullion to shape it into a curve, then add a 10-wrap Bullion from around the centre of the first Bullion towards the top on the other side of the bud. Refer to the design for the position of the Bullions.

Stems: The main stems and branches are worked in Stem Stitch. The stems of the buds are Couched.

Leaves: Some leaves on the sampler are Couched, others are very long Bullions. Refer to the table.

Design A	Thread	Needle	Stitch
Petals	Glory 6 and 17	Straw 7	Detached Chain Padding and Satin Stitch
		Long Darner 7	Bullion Stitch
Centres	Iris 24	Straw 7	Spider's Web
	Glory 69	Straw 7	Stem Stitch and French Knot
Stems	Iris 45	Straw 7	Stem Stitch
	Glory 45	Straw 7	Couching
Leaves	Iris 50	Straw 7	Couching
Design B			
Petals	Iris 107	Straw 7	Detached Chain Padding and Satin Stitch
		Long Darner 7	Bullion Stitch
Centres	Iris 45 (use brown only)	Straw 7	Spider's Web
	Glory 69	Straw 7	Stem Stitch and French Knot
Stems	Iris 45	Straw 7	Long Bullion Stitch, couched down
Design C			
Petals	Glory 17	Straw 7	Detached Chain Padding and Satin Stitch
		Long Darner	Bullion Stitch
Centres	Glory 17	Straw 7	Rings of Satin Stitch
Stems	Glory 45	Straw 7	Stem Stitch
Leaves	Glory 50	Straw 7	Couching
Design D			
Petals	Glory 94	Straw 7	Detached Chain Padding and Satin Stitch
Centres	Iris 120	Straw 7	Spider's Web
	Glory 69	Straw 7	Bullion Stitch (couched) and French Knot
Stems	Glory 110	Straw 7	Stem Stitch
Leaves	Glory 110	Straw 7	Couching
Buds	Glory 94	Straw 7	Satin Stitch and Bullion Stitch
Design E			
Petals	Iris 17 and 125	Straw 7	Detached Chain Padding and Satin Stitch
Centres	Iris 120	Straw 7	Spider's Web
	Glory 69	Straw 7	Bullion Stitch (couched) and French Knot
Stems	Iris 45 (use brown only)	Straw 7	Stem Stitch
Leaves	Glory 50	Straw 7	Couching
Buds	Iris 17	Straw 7	Satin Stitch

Antique Rose Sampler

*There's a delightful, old world charm about this reproduction
antique sampler. To personalise the design, change the
initials to ones significant to you.*

MATERIALS

- 60cm x 65cm (24in x 26in) ecru evenweave linen (12 threads per cm)

- DMC Stranded Embroidery Cotton: one skein each of very dark mahogany (300), black (310), very dark pistachio green (319), medium pistachio green (320), navy blue (336), dark terracotta (355), very light mahogany (402), light hazelnut brown (422), medium brown (433), very light brown (435), dark tan (437), light avocado green (470), dark blue green (501), dark fern green (520), very dark violet (550), dark drab brown (611), light drab brown (613), dark old gold (680), dark coffee brown (801), light garnet (814), medium garnet (815), dark navy blue (823), medium golden olive (831), ultra dark pistachio green (890), medium copper (920), dark antique blue (930), medium antique blue (931), dark khaki green (3011), very light mocha brown (3033), dark yellow beige (3045), medium yellow beige (3046), medium shell pink (3722), dark antique violet (3740), chocolate brown (3772), light terracotta (3778)

- No 24 or 26 tapestry needle

- Embroidery hoop or frame (optional)

STITCH USED

Cross Stitch

FINISHED SIZE

39cm x 42cm (15⅜in x 16½in)

PREPARATION

Hand-overcast, bind or overlock the raw edges of your linen to prevent it fraying. If you wish to start your embroidery in the centre, fold the linen in halves vertically and horizontally. Sew a line of running stitches along the folds, taking care to follow the same thread from side to side. The threads will intersect at the centre of the fabric. Find the centre of the design on the pattern sheet by counting the squares of the grid. Rule lines from top to bottom and side to side, intersecting at the centre of the design.

Alternatively, start stitching 11cm (4⅜in) in from the side and 11cm (4⅜in) from the top or bottom of the fabric.

STITCHING

Each square on the pattern sheet represents a Cross Stitch worked over two threads of linen. The symbol in each square indicates the colour to use.

You will note from the colour key on the pattern sheet that there are two symbols for some colours and that these are very similar. One symbol represents a stitch worked in two strands of a particular shade, the other symbol represents a stitch worked in one strand of the same shade.

Unless otherwise indicated, all the colours are worked in two strands. When working in two strands, the neatest and most economical way to start a thread is the loop method. Cut your thread twice the usual length, remove a single strand and thread the two cut ends of the strand into your needle. Take the needle and thread through the fabric from front to back, leaving a loop of thread on the right side. Bring the needle and thread to the front of the fabric, two threads to the right and two threads up, and take the needle through the loop before going back into the same hole, pulling the loop to the back of the work. Continue to stitch in the usual manner.

When working with a single strand, start stitching with a waste knot. Knot your thread and take the needle into the fabric from the front to the back, 2cm (⅝in) to the right of where you wish to begin. Bring your needle from the back to the front and stitch in the usual way, securing the beginning thread with several stitches. Cut off the knot.

To finish off a thread, weave it through the back of previous stitches and trim off any excess. Do not carry your thread across the back of the work for more than two or three stitches as it may show through to the right side and spoil the look of your finished work.

FINISHING

Before framing your finished embroidery, gently launder with mild soap and warm water. Swish the embroidery through the water without squeezing or rubbing. Rinse very well in warm or cold water and roll in a towel to absorb excess moisture.

To press, cover your ironing board with a light-coloured, fluffy towel and place embroidery right side down. Use a medium iron and avoid pressing too heavily or you may flatten the stitches. ✻

Goldwork Frog and Turtle

Dramatic black is the perfect background for this imaginative goldwork.
Designed and stitched by Jan Watts, these wonderful boxes
are embellished with a variety of Rajmahal gold threads.

MATERIALS

FOR EACH BOX:

- Rajmahal satin box, either large and round or a jewellery box
- 30cm (12in) square moiré taffeta for background fabric
- 30cm (12in) square voile
- 30cm (12in) square fusible webbing
- 5cm (2in) square deep-yellow felt
- 20cm (8in) embroidery hoop
- Polyester sewing thread: Gütermann No 968
- No 3, 8 and 10 crewel needles
- No 18 chenille needle
- Saral paper: yellow or white*
- Sharp white tailors' chalk pencil
- Greaseproof paper

BULRUSH FROG:

- Rajmahal Art Silk: one skein each of persimmon (144), maidenhair (521)
- 60cm (24in) Rajmahal Gold Pearl Sadi (fine)
- 4m (4³/₈yd) Rajmahal Gold Handsew Metal Thread
- 50cm (¹/₂yd) Rajcord
- 5cm (2in) Rajmahal Gold Check Sadi (fine)

WATERLILY TURTLE:

- Rajmahal Art Silk: one skein each of baby camel (45), maidenhair (521), verdigris (926)
- 40cm (16in) Rajmahal Gold Smooth Sadi (fine)
- 10cm (4in) Rajmahal Gold Pearl Sadi (fine)
- 3m (3³/₈yd) Rajmahal Gold Handsew Metal Thread

* Saral paper is used in folk art to transfer designs to wood – it is chalk-based, not wax-based as dressmaker's carbon is.

STITCHES USED

Couching, Satin Stitch, French Knots, Straight Stitch, Whip Stitch, Stab Stitch

GENERAL INSTRUCTIONS FOR BOTH DESIGNS

Read carefully through all instructions before commencing the work.

Prepare the fabric layers: Fuse the voile square to the back of the moiré taffeta with the webbing, making sure that the grain of each piece of fabric is straight.

Transferring the design (page 81) to the prepared fabric: Trace the design onto greaseproof paper, taking care to mark the centring lines. Mark the centre lines on the fabric by folding the fabric in half lengthwise and marking each end of the fold using the chalk pencil. Open the fabric and re-fold in half crosswise, aligning the previous marked lines. Mark each end of this fold using the chalk pencil.

Open the fabric out flat. Place the traced design onto the fabric, matching the centre lines. Pin across the top to hold in place. Slide the Saral paper under the greaseproof paper and trace the design. When all lines have been traced, remove the Saral paper. Check the design and then remove the tracing.

Mounting: Place the prepared fabric into the hoop, keeping the grain straight and the fabric taut.

STITCHING/ATTACHING THE SADI

Sadi thread is a coiled wire (gold or silver), spiralled into a very pliable hollow spring. Smooth Sadi is stitched to the fabric like a bead, the thread being taken through the spiral core. The Sadi itself is not taken through the fabric. Secure the thread on the wrong side of the work, bringing it through to the right side at the beginning of the 'bead' position. Carefully thread the cut Sadi

length onto a fine crewel needle and down the thread so that it sits flat on the fabric. Take the thread through to the wrong side at the end of the Sadi length. Bring the thread through to the right side at the beginning of the next Sadi bead position. Cut the next Sadi length and stitch it onto the fabric. Although it is a little more time consuming, a better result is achieved if each Sadi length is measured and cut after the previous piece has been stitched into position.

Pearl Sadi can be either stitched like a bead using a very fine needle or couched into position. If couching, you should run the stitching thread through beeswax to strengthen and smooth the thread prior to stitching. Position the cut length onto the work and take small stitches over the Sadi. The Sadi coil should open just enough to allow the working thread to slip between coils and 'disappear'.

STITCHING HANDSEW METAL THREAD

Use two lengths side by side. Leave an excess of approximately 7.5cm (3in) sitting on the right side, to be taken to the wrong side of the work and secured later. Secure the Handsew Metal Thread with small Couching stitches, taken at right angles to the thread, approximately 5-10mm (¹/₄-³/₈in) apart. It is important to keep your stitches evenly spaced on the straight areas of the design. The stitches will need to be closer together as you stitch around the curves, (diagram 1). To achieve smooth curves and particularly tight curves, position and stitch the inner thread first and then position the outer thread to sit smoothly against the inner line and stitch over the two threads. Always keep the two threads that are sitting flat side by side. Be careful not to

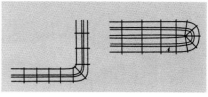

DIAGRAM 1

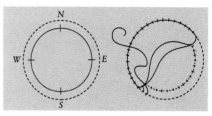

DIAGRAM 2

First layer: 2-3mm (^{1}/₈in) smaller than the second layer. Secure N, S, E and W positions first.

Second layer: Secure N, S, E and W positions first. Place stitches halfway between these. Keep halving the distance, stitching until the edge is smooth.

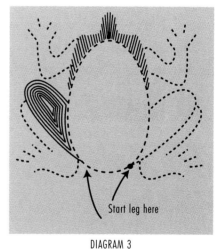

DIAGRAM 3

Stitch direction guide for the body and upper legs.

let them twist or overlap. When you reach the end and have made the last stitich, take the thread to the wrong side and secure on the back of the work. Place the No 18 chenille needle into the fabric at the end of the design line. Thread the end of the Handsew Metal Thread through the eye of the needle and take it through to the back of the work. Whip-stitch the end of the Metal Thread to the voile for 2-3cm (approximately 1in). Repeat for the other end of the Metal Thread. Clip off excess thread.

PADDING

Cut the felt into two pieces using the patterns provided. Position and stitch the smaller piece first. Only four stitches are needed to secure the first felt layer – one stitch each at points north, south, east and west.

Bring the needle up against the edge of the felt and take a small Stab Stitch down through the felt at each of these points. Position the second, larger piece of felt over the top of the secured first piece. Stitch at the same four points and then stitch halfway between each point. Keep halving the gaps and stitching until the felt is stitched smoothly in place. There should be no bumps at the edge of the felt (diagram 2).

BULRUSH FROG

Prepare the fabric layers, transfer the design, and mount the fabric into the hoop as described.

Body: Cut the two body pieces from the felt. Pad the body with the felt layers and cover using Pearl Sadi lengths. Work from the centre of the body out to one side. Return to the centre and complete the remaining half of the body. Stitch the first three coils and the last three coils of each length and then place extra stitches through the longer lengths of the frog's body.

Upper legs: Using a single strand of maidenhair (521) in a No 8 crewel needle, double the Handsew Metal

Thread and Couch in position. Begin at the lower point of the leg shape against the body, following the direction of the arrows in diagram 3. Work the outside shape first, then work a continuous line until the centre is reached, keeping the metal threads as close together as possible. It will take approximately seven rounds to fill the shape. The Couching stitches should be a maximum of 6mm (¼in) apart and much closer around the curves. Take the ends of the metal thread to the wrong side of the work and secure as described in the special instructions.

Lower arms and legs: Use a single line of doubled Handsew and Couch in position with a single strand of machine thread in a No 10 crewel needle.

Cut short lengths of Pearl Sadi for the toes and fingers and stitch in place with a single strand of machine thread in a No 10 crewel needle. Secure the stitching thread in place on the wrong side of the work.

Water lines: Couch the Rajcord along the water lines using a single strand of machine thread. Take the Rajcord through to the back of the work and stitch to secure.

Finishing the frog's body: Gently stretch a 7cm (2¾in) piece of Pearl Sadi coil to measure 18cm (7in). Use your machine thread to Couch the Pearl Sadi into position around the body, defining and neatening it. Continue around a second time. Secure the ends of the stretched Pearl Sadi and then stitch with machine thread on the wrong side of the work.

Use a single strand of maidenhair (521) in a No 10 crewel needle to Satin-stitch the remainder of the body shape. Begin at the centre top of the head and work down one side, then return to the centre top to complete the other side.

Eyes: Cut two lengths of 1cm (⅜in) from the Check Sadi and stitch in a circle for the eyes. Use six strands of persimmon (144) in a No 3 crewel needle to work a French Knot in the centre of the eye.

Bulrushes: Using a single strand of Handsew in a No 3 crewel needle, Straight-stitch the stems of the four bulrushes. Work a small securing thread in the centre of the bulrush position using the same thread. Cut a 1cm (⅜in) length of Check Sadi, thread onto a needle and stitch like a bead. Make the holding stitch slightly longer to give the bulrush a spike at the tip. Secure the metal thread on the back of the work.

WATERLILY TURTLE

Prepare the fabric, transfer the design and mount the fabric in the hoop as described in the general instructions.

Water lines: Using a No 18 chenille needle, bring a doubled length of Handsew through to the front of the work. With a single strand of verdigris (926) in a No 8 crewel needle, Couch the Handsew in position. Secure the metal thread firmly on the wrong side of the work.

Body: Cut the two felt body pieces and pad the body with felt as described in the general instructions. Use Smooth Sadi to fill the body shape, then begin in the centre of the body, filling one side and returning to the centre to complete the other side.

Cut two, 5cm (2in) lengths of Pearl Sadi. Stretch each piece to measure 10cm (4in). Couch the first piece of Pearl Sadi around the edge of the padded body using machine thread for the Couching.

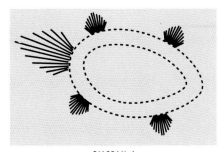

DIAGRAM 4
Satin stitch direction guide

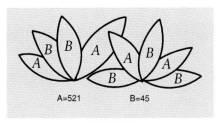

A=521   B=45

DIAGRAM 5
Waterlily colour placement

Trim to the exact length of the body, abut the ends together (but do not overlap) and secure the ends by taking several stitches over the first and last two coils.

Couch the second piece of stretched Pearl Sadi around the outer body shape in the same way.

Head and feet: Refer to diagram 4. Use a single strand of baby camel (45) in a No 8 crewel needle. Begin in the centre of the shape and Satin-stitch to one side, returning to the centre to complete the stitching. Cut two tiny 'beads' of Smooth Sadi and stitch in place for the eyes.

Waterlilies: Refer to diagram 5 for colour placement. Using a single strand of baby camel (45) or maidenhair (521), work the leaves in Satin Stitch. Again, begin in the centre of the shape, working one side and then the other.

Gardener's Delight

*Michelle Stieper has used stumpwork techniques to create this topiary tree
surrounded by beading and garlands of flowers. Amazingly,
only two embroidery stitches are used, making this a perfect project
for a first venture into raised embroidery.*

MATERIALS

- 30cm (12in) square ivory duchess satin or silk

- 30cm (12in) square quilter's muslin or calico

- 6cm (2½in) square 30-count silk mesh (petit point gauze)

- 20cm (8in) square calico for mounting the silk mesh

- DMC Stranded Embroidery Cottons: one skein each of dark hunter green (3345), hunter green (3346), yellow green (3347), dark beige brown (838), dark coffee brown (801), dark garnet (814), garnet (816), yellow (3820), dark yellow (3821), dark rust (918), rust (919), medium copper (920), light copper (921)

- DMC Soft Tapestry Cotton: one skein of dark beige (2640)

- Mill Hill beads: one packet each of red petite glass beads (42013), red frosted glass beads (62032), red glass seed beads (02013), brown frosted glass beads (62023)

- 10cm x 5cm (4in x 2in) green felt

- 10cm x 5cm (4in x 2in) fusible webbing

- Small handful of toy stuffing

- No 18 chenille needle

- No 10-13 beading needles

- No 5-10 crewel needles

- No 26 tapestry needle

- Rayon machine embroidery thread for tacking

- Tracing paper

- Tissue paper or greaseproof paper

- Fine (0.5mm) HB lead pencil

- Fine (0.2mm) Artline felt-tipped permanent marker

- Small sharp scissors

- 20cm (8in) wooden embroidery hoop

- Cotton tape or bias binding

FINISHED SIZE

13.5cm x 8.5cm (5¼in x 3¼in) (approximately)

STITCHES USED

Double Cast-on Stitch, Tent Stitch, French Knot, Buttonhole Stitch, Cast-on Stitch, Straight Stitch, Zig zag Stitch, Stab Stitch

PREPARATION

Bind the inner ring of the hoop with cotton tape or bias binding. Place the satin over the quilter's muslin or calico and mount together in the hoop. Pull both fabrics until they are drum tight. Tighten the screw well.

Using the the fine felt-tipped marker trace template A from the pattern (page 82) onto the tissue paper. Carefully centre the design on top of the satin and pin in place. Using the rayon machine embroidery thread, tack through the paper and fabric along the design lines, beginning and ending the tacking with secure knots. When complete, carefully tear the paper away.

Using the HB pencil, trace template B onto the tracing paper but do not trace letters A and B. On the reverse of the paper, carefully retrace over all the dots but not the broken lines of the pot and garlands. Turn the paper the correct side up and match the tracing with the tacked outline on the satin. Without moving the paper, carefully retrace over the dots, then remove the paper (the dots should now be transferred to the satin).

BEAD BORDER

Using one strand of embroidery cotton in garnet (816), begin each thread with a knot. Bring the needle up through one of the pencilled dots, thread on one red frosted glass bead (62032) followed by one red petite glass bead (42013). Take the needle down through the first frosted bead and back through the dot (diagram 1). Knot off well on the reverse side of the fabric. Apply the remaining beads in the same way. Always knot off after each dot and begin with a knot for

the next dot. Do not carry the thread over on the reverse of your work.

FLOWER GARLANDS

Refer to diagram 2. The figures on the diagram indicate the colour to use and the number of Cast-on Stitches. For example, the centre flower in the top garland is worked in two strands of dark garnet (814) with 16 Cast-on Stitches in each of the five petals.

Start stitching with the centre flower in the garland. Thread two strands of DMC cotton in the colour indicated into the No 6 crewel needle. Refer to the step-by-step instructions in diagram 3 for working the Double Cast-on Stitch petals. When working the flowers, always make a small backstitch on the wrong side of the fabric between each petal to prevent it retracting as the next petal is worked.

Work five petals for each flower in the order shown in diagram 4.

Complete each flower with a single-wrap French Knot in the centre using the No 9 crewel needle, two strands of yellow (3820) for the red flowers and two strands of dark yellow (3821) for the purple flowers.

Work the Double Cast-on Stitch leaves (12 cast-ons for each leaf) using two strands of hunter green (3346) or dark hunter green (3345) in the No 6 crewel needle.

TOPIARY TRUNK

Thread two strands of dark beige (2640) soft tapestry cotton into the No 18 chenille needle and knot the end. Bring the threaded needle up through point A.

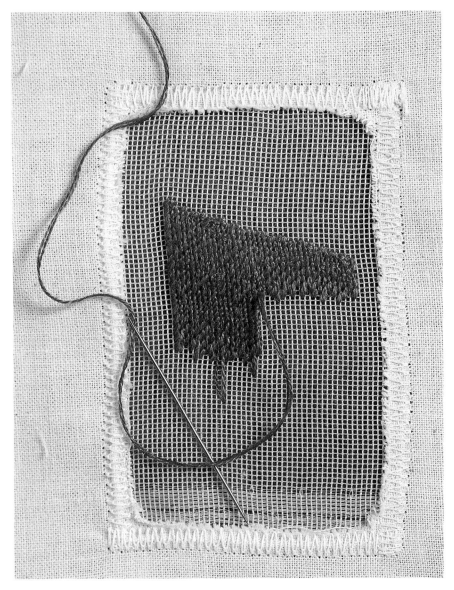

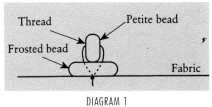

Thread · Petite bead · Frosted bead · Fabric

DIAGRAM 1

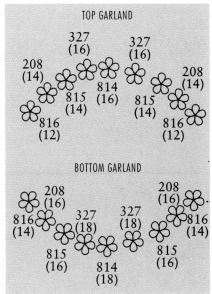

TOP GARLAND

327
(16) · 327
(16)

208
(14) · 208
(14)

814
(16)

815
(14) · 815
(14)

816
(12) · 816
(12)

BOTTOM GARLAND

208
(16) · 208
(16)

816
(14) · 816
(14)

327
(18) · 327
(18)

815
(16) · 815
(16)

814
(18)

DIAGRAM 2 — Garlands

Unthread the needle, knot the end of one long strand of dark beige brown (838) and thread it into the No 10 crewel needle. Also bring this thread up at point A.

Hold the soft tapestry cotton in your free hand. With your other hand, use the single strand of cotton to wrap the two strands of tapestry cotton. You will find it easiest to rest the hoop on a table while doing this. Wrap closely so that no soft cotton shows through. When the required length has been wrapped (the distance between A and B), thread all

three strands into the chenille needle and take it to the back of the fabric at point B. Knot off securely on the wrong side.

TOPIARY HEAD

Using the HB pencil, trace the three circles from diagram 5 onto the paper side of the webbing and attach it to the felt by ironing it on, paper side up. Carefully cut out the circles and remove the paper.

DIAGRAM 3 – Double Cast-on Stitch

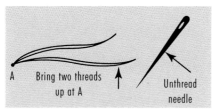

STEP 1: This stitch is best worked in a hoop. Thread two strands of thread into needle. Make a small knot or small stitch to secure thread. Bring threaded needle through the fabric at A. Once the threads are completely pulled through, unthread the needle.

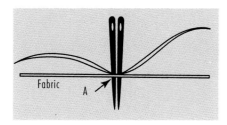

STEP 2: Insert the needle, plus a second needle of equal size, into point A. Insert both needles approximately one-third of their length into the fabric. Lay one thread to one side of the needles, the second thread to the other side.

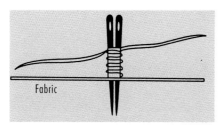

STEP 3: Work Buttonhole Stitches over both needles, alternating first one thread then the other. These are the 'cast-ons'.

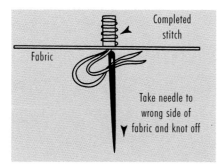

STEP 4: When the desired number of cast-ons have been made, carefully remove one needle. Thread both threads into the remaining needle and carefully pull the needle through to the wrong side of the fabric. Knot off the threads on the wrong side of the fabric.

Centre circle 1, with the webbing facing upwards, over the trunk. Using one strand of dark hunter green (3345) in the No 10 crewel needle, stitch the circle in place with small Stab Stitches. Stitch circle 2 over the first circle, then top these with circle 3. When the three circles have been Stab-stitched in place, Buttonhole-stitch around the outer edge of circle 3 (see the step-by-step photographs).

The topiary head is completed by filling the area with Double Cast-on Stitches, using two strands of DMC stranded cotton in the colours indicated. Each leaf has 12 or 14 cast-ons. Begin by working Cast-on Stitches around the outer edge in two strands of dark hunter green (3345) (see the step-by-step photographs).

Continue gradually working inwards, using increasingly lighter shades, as follows:

Two strands of dark hunter green (3345) for two rounds.

One strand of dark hunter green (3345) and one strand of hunter green (3346) for three rounds.

Two strands of hunter green (3346) for three rounds.

One strand of hunter green (3346) and one strand of yellow green (3347) to fill the remainder of the shape.

Once the leaves have been completed, add the beads. Using one strand of the garnet (816) thread and the No 10 crewel needle, apply approximately 24 red frosted glass beads (62032) around the outer area of the topiary head, then add approximately seven red glass seed beads (02013) in the centre. Knot the thread and bring the needle through the fabric and felt, drop on a bead and take the needle back through the felt and fabric into roughly the same hole. Some beads will almost completely disappear among the leaves, others will be more visible.

TERRACOTTA POT

Centre the silk mesh onto the square of calico. Machine-stitch the mesh to the calico around the outer edge of the mesh using Straight Stitch followed by a close Zigzag stitch. Turn the calico over and, without cutting into the silk mesh or stitching, carefully cut away the calico backing the mesh area.

Using the No 26 tapestry needle, stitch the terracotta pot following the graph on the pattern sheet. Each square on the graph represents one Tent Stitch and each symbol indicates the appropriate colour. Use one strand each of the shades indicated in the colour key.

Begin stitching by securing the thread under the back of the first few stitches, and end off by weaving the cotton through the back of the previously worked stitches.

When the stitching has been completed, cut out the pot leaving a 5mm (¼in) seam allowance all around. Using one strand of dark rust (918) in the No 10 crewel needle, stitch the seam allowance to the wrong side of the embroidered pot. Clip the corners and stitch the seam allowance in the order indicated in diagram 6.

Still using one strand of dark rust (918) and the No 10 crewel needle, stitch the pot to the satin where indicated by the tacked outline. Secure the pot with small Stab Stitches at each corner first, then Stab-stitch firstly down the left side, then the right side and finally across the bottom. The top is left open. Ideally the Stab Stitches should be invisible. To achieve this, bring the needle up through the satin (following the tacked outline) and then on the return journey just catch the edge of the embroidered pot with the needle before going back into the same hole in the satin. Once the pot is applied it should stand away from the satin.

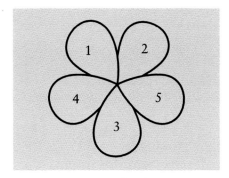

DIAGRAM 4 — Working the petals

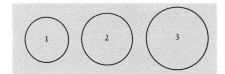

DIAGRAM 5 — Topiary head templates

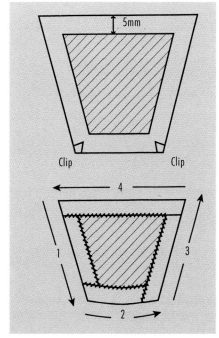

DIAGRAM 6 — Applying terracotta pot.

Lightly fill the pot with toy stuffing until almost (but not quite) full. Using one strand of dark coffee brown (801) in the No 10 crewel needle, lightly stitch the stuffing in place but don't pull too tightly. Using one strand of dark coffee brown (801) in the beading needle, begin stitching the brown frosted glass beads (62023) in place. Each bead is stitched individually, building up the beads until the pot is full (the framed sample used approximately 230 beads). Knot the threads securely. ❀

Patterns

BLUE AND WHITE ROSE – GRAPH

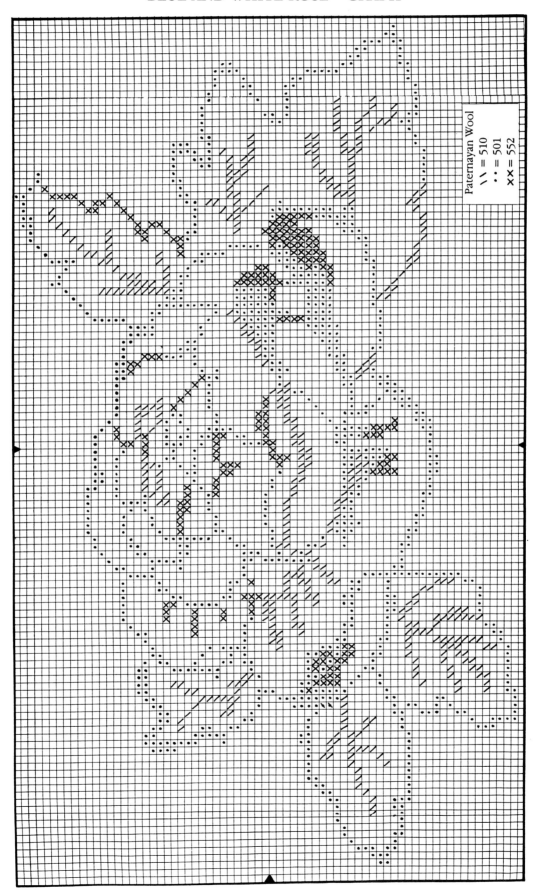

WOOL EMBROIDERED BASKET

EMBROIDERY OUTLINE FOR LID

EMBROIDERY OUTLINE
FOR PIN CUSHION

CHRISTMAS BUSH ENVELOPE BAG

EMBROIDERY DESIGN
ACTUAL SIZE

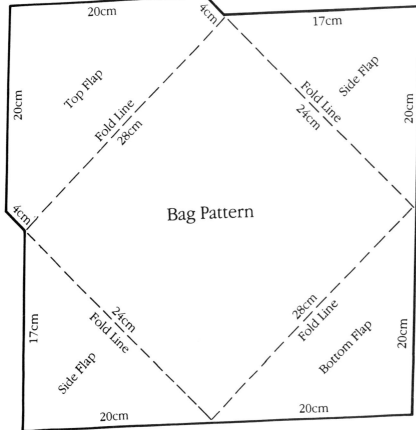

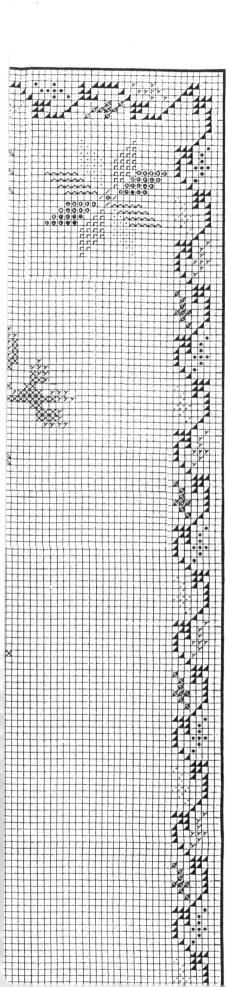

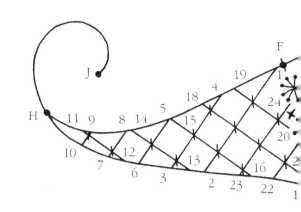

Stitch Key
Use chenille needle un

Petals

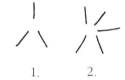

1.   2.

		10cm	10cm
1.2m	Back	10cm	Side Front
		Side Front	
	85cm		
10cm	Top Front		
10cm	Base Front		
	Flounce 1		
	Flounce 2		
	Flounce 3		
14cm each	Flounce 4		

2.5m

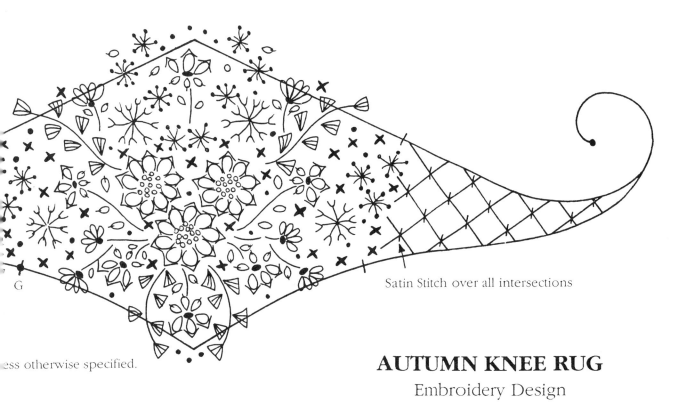

G

Satin Stitch over all intersections

...ess otherwise specified.

AUTUMN KNEE RUG
Embroidery Design

Large Daisy

Petals - nine petals worked with Satin Stitch
(two strands 872, three times over into same
hole. Work petals in order shown.
Work nine French Knots in the centre
(one strand 292 using straw needle).
Work one Satin Stitch (one strand 292)
between each petal, running two-thirds
of the way from the base of the petal.
Work an open Fly Stitch at the end
of each petal (one strand 702).

3.

Fly Stitch Flowers

Nine petals. Work Fly Stitches on the end of a
Satin Stitch (one strand 461). Make petals different
lengths. Centre, small Satin Stitch flower - four
petals worked in Satin Stitch three times over into
the same holes (one strand 461).

Pistil Stitch Flowers

Nine petals. Pistil Stitch (one strand 222 using
straw needle). French Knot flower centre
(one strand 292 using straw needle).

Buttonhole Flowers

Work two Buttonhole Stitches into the same
hole for each flower (one strand 712).
Stem in Stem Stitch (one strand 343).

B

Satin Stitches

Bud

GOLDWORK TURTLE AND FROG

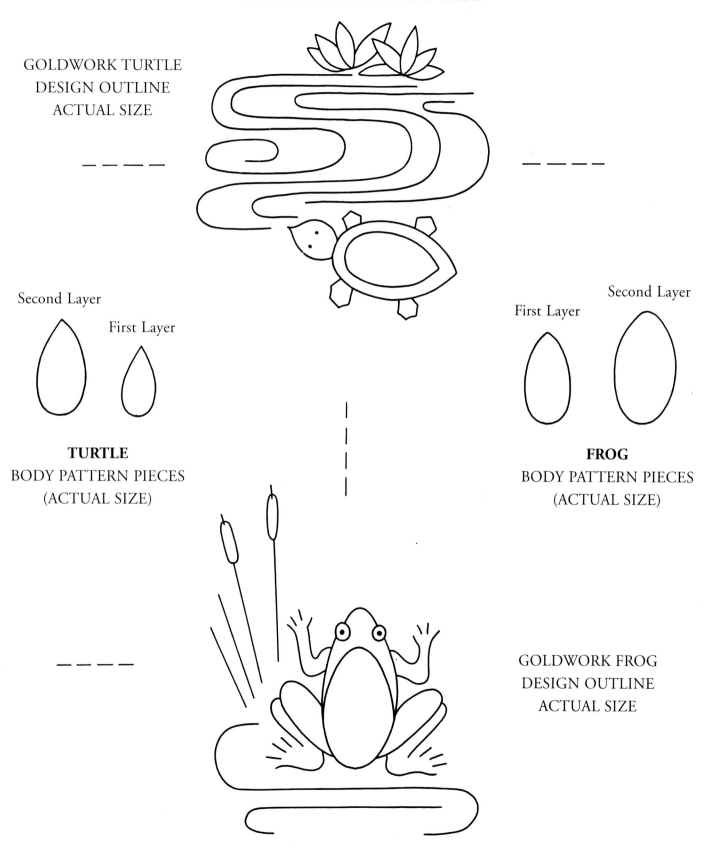

GOLDWORK TURTLE
DESIGN OUTLINE
ACTUAL SIZE

Second Layer

First Layer

TURTLE
BODY PATTERN PIECES
(ACTUAL SIZE)

First Layer

Second Layer

FROG
BODY PATTERN PIECES
(ACTUAL SIZE)

GOLDWORK FROG
DESIGN OUTLINE
ACTUAL SIZE

GARDENER'S DELIGHT

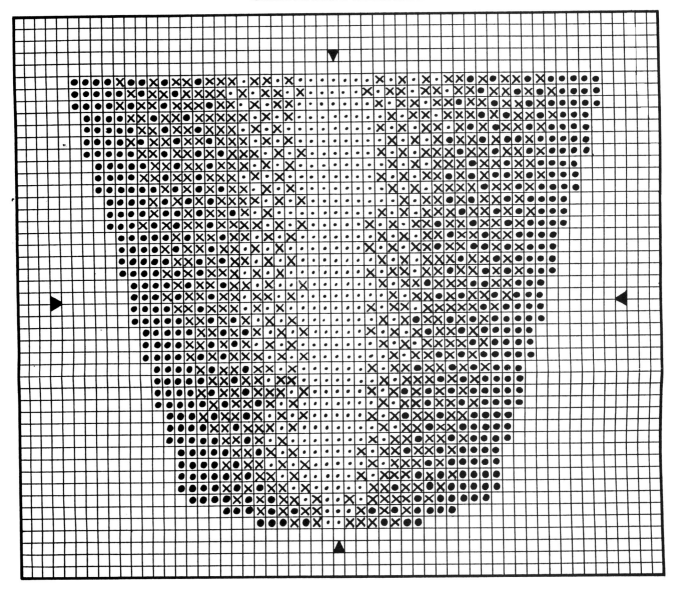

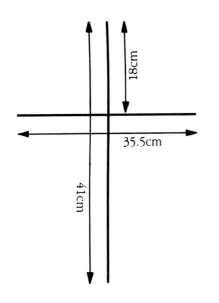

TERRACOTTA POT GRAPH

KEY

DMC STRANDED COTTON

◉ = 918/919

☒ = 919/920

⊡ = 920/921

GERALDTON WAX SAMPLER

DESIGN OUTLINE
ACTUAL SIZE

HEARTS & RIBBONS BASSINETTE SET

SHEET EMBROIDERY DESIGN

PILLOWCASE EMBROIDERY DESIGN

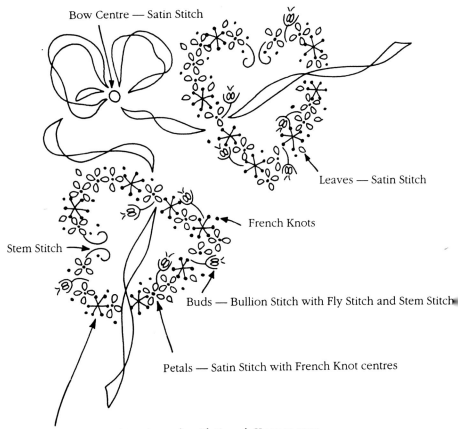

Bow Centre — Satin Stitch

Leaves — Satin Stitch

Stem Stitch

French Knots

Buds — Bullion Stitch with Fly Stitch and Stem Stitch

Petals — Satin Stitch with French Knot centres

Star Flowers — Pistil Stitch petals with French Knot centres

TEDDY BEAR COATHANGERS

ANGEL BEAR
EMBROIDERY DESIGN
ACTUAL SIZE

GARLANDED BEAR
EMBROIDERY DESIGN
ACTUAL SIZE

Stitch Guide

Silk Ribbon Stitches

FOLDED RIBBON ROSES

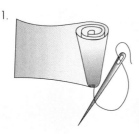

1: Fold the raw edges down a little, then roll the ribbon three or four times to form the centre of the rose. Secure with three or four stitches.

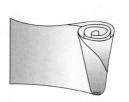

3: Pull the centre of the rose down so when you roll it into the ribbon, it will be level with the top of the fold. Stitch the base of the rose after each fold.

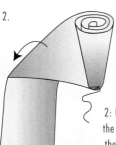

2: Fold the ribbon on the cross. Each fold of the ribbon is a petal.

4: Keep folding and stitching until all of the ribbon has been used. To finish, stitch the ribbon at the bottom of the rose to prevent fraying.

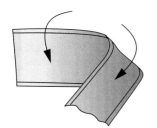

RIBBON LEAVES

RIBBON STITCH

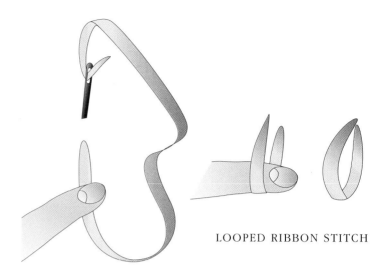

LOOPED RIBBON STITCH

SIDE RIBBON STITCH

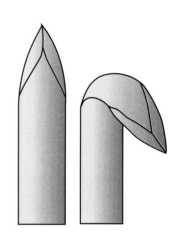

JAPANESE RIBBON STITCH

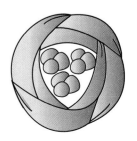

EXTENDED RIBBON STITCH

STRAIGHT STITCH ROSE

Embroidery Stitches

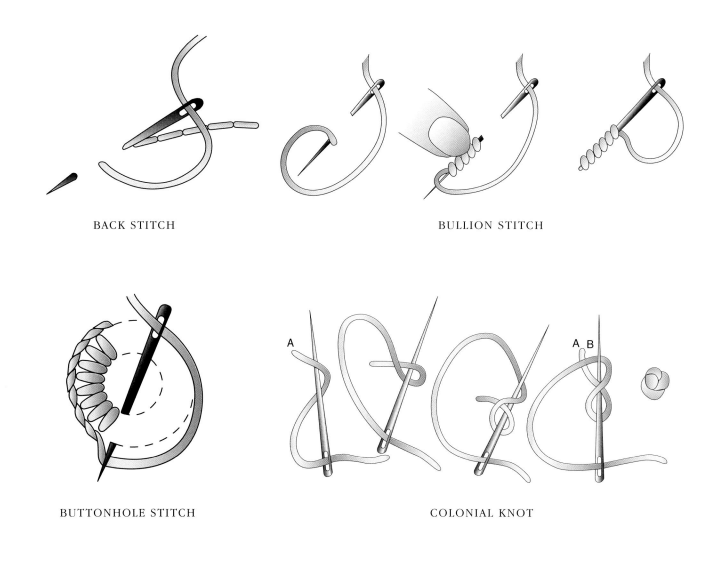

BACK STITCH

BULLION STITCH

BUTTONHOLE STITCH

COLONIAL KNOT

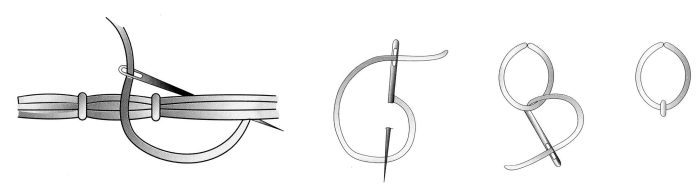

COUCHING STITCH

DETACHED CHAIN STITCH (LAZY DAISY STITCH)

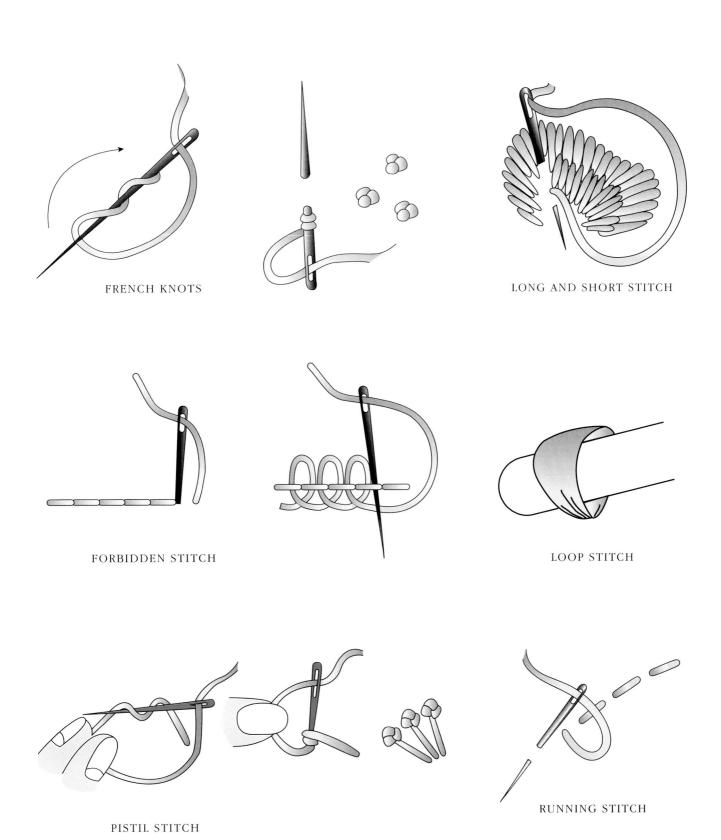

FRENCH KNOTS

LONG AND SHORT STITCH

FORBIDDEN STITCH

LOOP STITCH

PISTIL STITCH

RUNNING STITCH

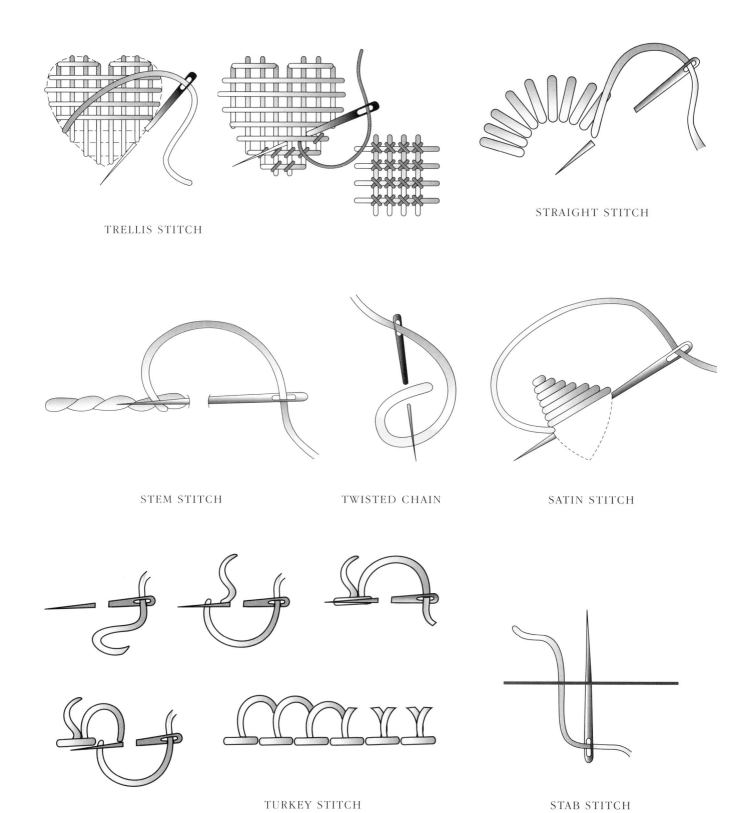

TRELLIS STITCH

STRAIGHT STITCH

STEM STITCH

TWISTED CHAIN

SATIN STITCH

TURKEY STITCH

STAB STITCH

The Basic Essentials

The right tools are essential for any job – needlework is no different. There are a few essentials and some optional extras that every needleworker should have.

SCISSORS

❖

Buy the best that you can afford and look after them. Good scissors will last for a lifetime. Look for scissors that can be unscrewed and sharpened professionally. Never, ever cut paper with scissors intended to cut fabric or thread. In fact, don't use them to cut anything but fabric or thread. Make sure the family knows that the scissors are not for general use. Embroidery scissors should have fine blades tapering to sharp points. You will use them for cutting threads close to the fabric. Take care not to damage the points by dropping the scissors. A scissor ball is a good idea. This is a small weight that attaches to the handles and ensures that the ball and not the points land first if the scissors are dropped. A good pair of dressmaking scissors for cutting fabric is a good idea. These should have long blades and comfortable handles. It is a good idea to buy or make a sheath in which to store the scissors when not in use.

FABRIC MARKERS

❖

There is a wide range of markers available. Some use permanent ink which will not wash out. Others are temporary markers – some are water-errasable and others fade with exposure to light. Before marking out a design, consider which variety will best suit your purpose. Markings made by pens that fade with light may disappear before your project is finished. A water-soluble marker may not be suitable for use on a

fabric that cannot be washed. Always test your chosen marker on a scrap of fabric before marking out a whole design.

THIMBLES

❖

Some embroiderers can't take a stitch without one, others won't wear them. Thimbles are a matter of personal preference. They range from the economy models to sterling silver and gold-plated keepsakes. There are also ornamental thimbles which are designed to be admired rather than used.

Thimbles are particularly useful when working on heavy fabrics.

STILETTOS

❖

Also called an awl. This is a sharp-pointed instrument used to make a hole in heavy or stiff fabric. Useful in ribbon embroidery to allow the ribbon to pass through the fabric without being crushed.

NEEDLES

❖

There are many, many needles and all are designed for a specific purpose. It is important to use the correct needle for the particular technique you are working. The size of the needle is governed by the

thickness of the thread used. As a general rule, the thread should fit smoothly through the eye. Instructions usually specify the size and type of needle to use and you should follow the recommendations for the best possible result. Needle numbers refer to the size of the needle. The larger the number, the finer the needle. The most commonly used embroidery needles are crewel, chenille, straw or milliners' and tapestry needles.

Crewel needles are the most frequently used embroidery needles. They have a sharp point so they can easily pierce the fabric and a long slim eye to take one or more threads of stranded cotton or wool. They come in sizes 1 to 10.

Straw or milliners' needles are long and the same width along the entire length of the shank. They are particularly suitable for bullion and knot stitches. They have a small, round eye which is easy to thread. Sizes range from 1 to 9.

Chenille needles have a sharp point and long eye, making them perfect for working thicker threads and particularly suitable for candlewicking and ribbon embroidery. They come in sizes 13 to 26.

Tapestry needles have a blunt point and are most frequently used for canvaswork and cross stitch on evenweave fabrics. The blunt point passes easily through the holes in the canvas or fabric and is unlikely to pierce any thread sharing a common hole. They are also used in whipped stitches as they will slip between the fabric and stitch without snagging on the fabric. Sizes range 18 to 26.

FABRICS

Linen, cotton, homespun or calico, silk, satin, damask and even lightweight fabrics like voile are suitable for hand embroidery. The purpose of the finished embroidery determines which fabric to use. Basically, the fabric must have enough body to support the weight of the embroidery and the weave should be firm enough to hold the thread.

A sheer fabric like voile requires a fine thread. Care must be taken to avoid threads on the back showing through to the front and casuing a shadow effect.

Another point to consider when choosing fabric is whether your fabric has a matt or shiny finish and whether there is sufficient contrast between the fabric and the threads to be used.

Linen, calico and damask can be laundered. Silk and satin may require dry-cleaning. Any fabric with a tendency to fray - linen and silk, particularly - should be overlocked or hand overcast before you commence your embroidery. An alternative is to use an anti-fray product.

Velvet and velveteen offer a rich background, particularly for ribbon embroidery. Dress-weight fabrics have a base cloth that is not too closely woven and allows the ribbon to pass through easily. When working with threads on plush fabrics, care must be taken that the thread is thick enough to sit on the surface of the pile and not disappear into it.

Wool, cotton and linen are all suitable for embroidery with either ribbon or thread. Look for fabrics that are woven firmly enough to hold the threads. If using a loosely woven fabric you may need to add a backing to stabilise it and to prevent the stitches on the reverse side showing through to the front.

Silk is a luxurious background for special projects; moiré, dupion, Thai silk, taffeta, shot taffeta and satin are all suitable weights for framed pictures, cushions, clothing and fashion accessories.

THREADS

Stranded cottons, sometimes called floss, are probably the most popular of all embroidery threads. They come in an extensive range of colours and, although most are colour fast, it is a good idea to test for fastness if you are making an item that will require washing. Stranded cottons are composed of six threads and can be used whole or separated into the number of strands required. If separating, cut the required length, then separate one length at a time. Hold up the thread and allow it to untwist before putting together the number of threads you require. This helps the thread to sit well on the fabric and prevents twisting and tangling. You can also blend two or more colours to create subtle shading. Stranded cottons come in a range of plain colours and variegated shades.

There are also stranded threads in pure silk and synthetics. These have a rich lustre and can be used whole, separated or blended as for stranded cottons.

Rayon threads are used for Brazilian embroidery and have a lustrous finish. They need to be handled differently from other threads and instructions for Brazilian embroidery projects usually include this information.

Wools come in tapestry and crewel weights. If a finer wool is needed, use crewel wool rather than trying to split tapestry wool. Both come in a huge range of colours.

Perlé or pearl thread is a pure cotton two-ply, twisted to produce a beaded effect. Available in weights from a thick No 3 through the middleweights, No 5 and 8, to a fine No 12. These have a good lustre and come in a wide colour range but not all colours are available in all weights.

Hand-dyed threads are available in wool, silk and cotton, in both plain colours and overdyes. If the project is likely to require more than one skein of these threads, make sure you purchase the same dyelot. Being hand-dyed, the colours may vary between the various dye lots.

RIBBONS

Pure silk ribbon is soft and pliable, with a surface that looks the same on both sides. Available in widths from 2mm up to 32mm with the most used widths being 2mm, 4mm and 7mm.

Sheer ribbons, such as the synthetic organdies, can be used alone or in combination with another ribbon. They can be used to create shadow effects that lend perspective to your work and are suitable for folding as well as embroidery.

Synthetic ribbons made of 100 per cent Azlon look like silk ribbons, but have more spring than silk and will not lie as flat against the fabric. Available in 3.5mm and 7mm widths in a wide range of plain colours. There is also a range of Azlon ombre ribbon in the 3.5mm width and a picot-edged 6mm polyester ombre ribbon. Plain polyester ribbons come in many colours and widths.

Double-sided polyester satin comes in widths from 1.5mm to 90mm. Heavier and shinier than silk ribbon, it is suitable for making folded roses, concertina roses, free-form flowers and leaves. The narrowest satin ribbon can be couched to form branches and stems. The use of a stiletto is recommended if you wish to use polyester satin ribbon for embroidery.

Thread Conversion Chart

(Approximate colour conversions for DMC Stranded Cotton,
Anchor Stranded Cotton and Semco Stranded Cotton)

DMC	ANCHOR	SEMCO	DMC	ANCHOR	SEMCO	DMC	ANCHOR	SEMCO	DMC	ANCHOR	SEMCO
Blanc	2	998	524	858*	943	791	178	884	946	332*	822
Ecru	387	981	535	(1041)	987	792	941	881	947	330	822
208	111	869	543	933	978	793	176	880	948	1011	966
209	109	869	550	101	871	794	175	879	950	4146	967
210	108	868	552	99	870	796	133	891	951	1010	957
211	342	867	553	98	869	797	132	881	954	203	928
221	897*	971	554	(96)	868	798	131	890	955	206*	927
223	895	859	561	212	917	799	136	888	956	54	851
224	893	858	562	210	916	800	144	887	957	50*	843
225	026	840	563	208	915	801	359	975	958	187*	910
300	352	964	564	206*	912	806	(168)*	900	959	186*	909
301	1049	963	580	(281)*	951	807	168*	905	961	76*	854
304	1006	846	581	280*	950	809	130	888	962	75*	843
307	289	800	597	(168)*	905	813	161*	894	963	73	840
309	42	855	598	(167)*	902	814	45	857	964	185	908
310	403	999	600	78	856	815	43	849	966	(206)*	927
311	148	907	601	(63)	852	816	1005*	846	970	(316)*	818
312	979	896	602	57	847	817	13*	845	971	316*	818
315	1019	859	603	62	851	818	23	840	972	298	809
316	1017	859	604	55	850	819	271	823	973	297	804
317	400	987	605	(50)*	850	820	134	884	975	355	964
318	399	986	606	335	829	822	390	981	976	1001	962
319	218	918	608	332	822	823	(152)*	885	977	1002	961
320	215	928	610	889	984	824	164	891	986	246	918
321	9046	845	611	898	983	825	162*	896	987	244	934
322	978	889	612	832	982	826	161*	895	988	243	933
326	59	848	613	831	982	827	160	893	989	242	928
327	100	870	632	936	964	828	9159	892	991	(189)	917
333	119	877	640	(903)*	984	829	906	956	992	187*	916
334	977	889	642	392	983	830	277*	956	993	186*	919
335	38	843	644	830	981	831	(277)*	955	995	410	-
336	150	885	645	273	987	832	907*	955	996	433	-
340	118	876	646	8581*	987	833	(907)*	955	3011	845*	951
341	117	879	647	1040	986	834	874	954	3012	844	945
347	1025	846	648	900	986	838	380	976	3013	842	944
349	13*	835	666	46	835	839	(360)*	976	3021	905	988
350	(11)	831	676	891	811	840	379	980	3022	8581*	983
351	10	839	677	886	954	841	378	979	3023	(899)	982
352	9	830	680	901	813	842	376	978	3024	397	985
353	6	832	699	923*	914	844	1041*	988	3031	360*	976
355	1014	971	700	228	914	869	944	973	3032	903*	983
356	5975	969	701	227	929	890	(683)*	918	3033	391	981
367	217	924	702	226	929	891	35	844	3041	871	990
368	214	927	703	238	938	892	28	836	3042	870	989
369	1043	926	704	(256)*	932	893	41	843	3045	888	955
370	855	956	712	926	805	894	26	843	3046	887	954
371	854	955	718	88	865	895	1044	918	3047	852	953
372	853	954	720	326	963	898	360*	976	3051	681	946
400	351	964	721	324	818	899	52	851	3052	869	945
402	1047	965	722	323	965	900	333	831	3053	858*	944
407	914	980	725	305	808	902	897*	857	3064	883	980
413	401	992	726	295	803	904	258	934	3052	859*	945
414	235	987	727	293	802	905	257	934	3072	(847)	985
415	398	989	729	890	812	906	256*	942	3078	292	802
420	374	960	730	845	951	907	255	941	3325	129	887
422	943	958	731	924	952	909	(923)*	914	3326	36	842
433	371	974	732	281*	952	910	230	913	3328	1024	839
434	310*	973	733	280*	952	911	205	913	3340	329	827
435	1046	960	734	279	949	912	209	913	3341	328	826
436	1045	959	738	361	958	913	204	912	3345	268*	946
437	362	958	739	366	957	915	1029	866	3346	267*	933
444	290	804	740	316*	818	917	89	865	3347	266	932
445	288	800	741	304	816	918	341	971	3348	264	931
451	233	990	742	303	809	919	340	969	3350	65	855
452	232	989	743	302	808	920	1004	970	3354	74	853
453	231	989	744	301	807	921	(884)	963	3362	263	-
469	267*	951	745	300	806	922	1003	965	3363	262	945
470	267*	951	746	275	805	924	851	907	3364	(260)	977
471	266*	945	747	158	898	926	850	906	3371	382	977
472	(253)	948	754	1012	967	927	848	986	3607	87	864
498	(1005)*	846	758	9575	968	928	274	985	3608	86	863
500	683	921	760	1022	838	930	1035	897	3609	85	857
501	878	924	761	1021	837	931	1034	895	3685	1028	855
502	876	920	762	234	886	932	1033	894	3687	68	857
503	875	919	772	259	939	934	862*	947	3688	66	859
504	1042	922	775	128	892	935	861	947	3689	49	850
517	162*	896	776	24	842	936	846	947	3705	35*	834
518	1039	895	778	968	858	937	268*	947	3706	33	836
519	1038	893	780	(310)*	960	938	381	977	3708	31	842
520	862*	947	781	309	813	939	152*	895			
522	860	923	782	308	813	943	188	911			
523	859	944	783	307	812	945	881	966			

Index

Published by Craftworld Books

A division of Express Publications Pty Ltd ACN 057 807 904

Under licence from EP Investments Pty Ltd ACN 003 109 055 (1995)

2 Stanley Street Silverwater NSW 2128 Australia

First published by Craftworld Books 2000

Publisher Roslyn Smith

Photographic Director Robyn Wilson

Editor Roslyn Smith

Production Editors Nina Paine / Gabrielle Baxter

Designer Caroline Milne

National Library of Australia Cataloguing-in-Publication data

Creative Embroidery

Includes Index

ISBN 1 875625 240

1. Embroidery

Printed by KHL Printing

Australian distribution to newsagents by Network Distribution Company, 54 Park Street, Sydney NSW 2000, phone (02) 9282 8777

Australian book shop distribution by Gary Allen Book Distribution, 9 Cooper Street, Smithfield NSW 2164. Phone (02) 9725 2933

Overseas distribution enquiries to Godfrey Vella, phone (02) 9748 0599, Locked Bag 111, Silverwater NSW 1811 Australia

Email: gvella@expresspublications.com.au